Carl Sagan

Superstar Scientist

Carl Sagan

Superstar Scientist

Daniel Cohen

Illustrated with photographs

DODD, MEAD & COMPANY
New York

To Joe Ann Daly—for many years of good advice, confidence, patience, and friendship

 Distributed in Canada by McClelland and Stewart Limited, Toronto. Manufactured in the United States of America.

1 2 3 4 5 6 7 8 9 10

Library of Congress Cataloging-in-Publication Data
Cohen, Daniel. Carl Sagan: superstar scientist.
Bibliography: p. Includes index. Summary: A career biography of a celebrity scientist who has brought astronomy to books, magazines, and television, as to his Cornell University classroom. 1. Sagan, Carl, 1934– —Juvenile literature.
2. Astronomers—United States—Biography—Juvenile literature.
[1. Sagan, Carl, 1934– . 2. Astronomers] I. Title. QB36.S15C64 1987
520'.92'4 [B] [92] 87–6719
ISBN 0–396–08776–0

NOTE

I would like to acknowledge the generous help of Dr. Carl Sagan in preparing this manuscript. Not only did Dr. Sagan supply me with enormous quantities of material, he also took the time to read over what I had written, and very politely point out the places where I had gone astray in fact and interpretation. This book could never have been done without his aid. But while Dr. Sagan has been extremely cooperative, he is not responsible for what I have written. Whatever errors of fact and interpretation that may remain, or have been introduced in later drafts, are mine, and mine alone.

—Daniel Cohen

CONTENTS

INTRODUCTION

"Heeere's Carl!"

Sometimes when Carl Sagan would enter a classroom at Cornell University where he is Professor of Astronomy and Space Sciences, a student in the class would shout out: "Heeere's Carl!" in imitation of the famous opening line of the Johnny Carson "Tonight" show, "Heeere's Johnny!" Such a greeting may seem out of place in a university class, but in this case it's curiously appropriate.

Carl Sagan is probably the most famous scientist in the world today. His face, which is familiar to most TV viewers and has appeared on dozens of magazine covers, is instantly recognizable throughout the world. Carl Sagan imitations are a standard part of the routine of many impressionists. That is an honor awarded only the very famous, for it is pointless to do an impression of someone the audience will not recognize. Johnny Carson himself has been known to don a Carl Sagan wig and do an imitation. All this fame is for a man who has spent his entire adult life in a variety of academic positions. In a sense, Carl Sagan has never left school.

There have been other celebrity scientists—Albert Einstein, Madame Marie Curie, Jonas Salk—but they have been famous primarily for their scientific accomplishments. Sagan has no theory of relativity, no radium, no polio vaccine to his credit. He is a fine scientist with an exceptionally broad range of interests and accomplishments. He has published a prodigious number of scientific papers, many of them extremely important. He would have always been a celebrity among his scientific colleagues. But his scientific accomplishments do not explain his immense popularity with the general public. Most of us do not read articles that have titles like "Ultraviolet-Photoproduced Organic Solids Synthesized Under Simulated Jovian Conditions: Molecular Analysis." That is a Sagan article that appeared in the journal *Science.* We would not even be aware that such an article existed, and if we did happen to read it, we probably wouldn't understand it. The world of scientific literature is largely closed to the nonscientist.

But when Sagan writes an article for the mass-circulation Sunday supplement, *Parade,* or one of his books tops the best-seller list or wins a Pulitzer Prize, then the general public begins to take notice.

However, it is not his scientific or popular writings that have made Carl Sagan the scientist celebrity that he is. His fame comes mainly from television. Even in his undergraduate days Sagan was known as an excellent lecturer and enthusiastic popularizer of science. Early in his career he had written some popular articles and books. His first completely nontechnical book was *Planets,* published in 1966 as part of a Time-Life science book series. Back in 1968, he'd even written and narrated a TV series. Sagan has a voice many professional announcers would envy. But what really catapulted the young scientist into public view was his appearance on the "Tonight" show in 1972. Sagan was still a relatively obscure astronomer who had just written a book called *The Cosmic Connection,* a collection of brief, thoughtful pieces, generally centering around the theme of the possibility of contacting extraterrestrial intelligences. That was clearly a popular, even a sensational, topic.

Sagan had appeared on the TV show hosted by Dick Cavett, generally considered the most cerebral of talk show hosts. Carson happened to see the interview, liked what he saw, and contacted Sagan.

Sagan's publishers were naturally delighted. The "Tonight" show is where many hopeful authors have gone to hawk their wares. But success on the Carson show is by no means assured. Lots of Carson's guests have never been heard from again. As an unknown, at least as far as Johnny Carson's audience was concerned, Sagan was allotted a mere five minutes at the end of the show. He used his time very well, and proved to be so popular that Carson, who is a bit of an astronomy buff himself, invited the astronomer back three weeks later to talk about whatever he wished.

Sagan's second appearance on the "Tonight" show was, according to one writer, "One of the great reckless solos of late night television." His subject was nothing less than the history of the universe itself. "Fifteen billion years ago the Universe was without form. There were no galaxies, stars, or planets. There was no life. There was darkness everywhere," he began. According to *Time* magazine, "When Sagan's soliloquy ended, said a reviewer, 100,000 teenage listeners must have vowed on the spot to become astronomers."

It was certainly not the usual sort of fare for TV talk shows, but it worked. It captivated the audience and after that Sagan became something of a regular on the "Tonight" show, hence the student's greeting, "Heeere's Carl!"

Sagan's TV talents, his skill in communicating both information and enthusiasm are only half the story of his fame. The other half is the nature of his scientific interests. Since graduate school, his driving interest has been the exploration of other planets. But within that interest is an older love, one carried over from childhood, and one that most of us share: The possibility of finding life on other worlds. Perhaps the nature of the atmosphere of Jupiter does not really excite us, but the chance of finding other life forms on some distant planet, that's a thought that grabs every one of us. We have all speculated about the possibility. Sagan has done more than speculate. He was a pioneer in what has come to be called exobiology, the study of possible life elsewhere in the Universe. He did this at a time when the whole idea of finding life on other planets was deemed to be solely the realm of science fiction writers, not *real* scientists. Sagan pushed, prodded, inspired, and sometimes irritated his scientific colleagues into taking the subject seriously. He wasn't the only enthusiast for extraterrestrial life in the scientific community, but he was certainly the most visible and outspoken member of a small group.

Sagan had arrived on the scene at just the right moment. The U.S. space program was really getting underway. Satellites were being sent into space and concrete plans were being laid for reaching the moon and at least some of the nearby planets. Even though most scientists felt that the possibility of actually finding extraterrestrial life in the foreseeable future was extremely remote, the search could begin.

"I think myself extraordinarily fortunate to be alive at the one moment in the history of mankind when such ventures are being undertaken," Sagan has said.

Soon Sagan became known as an expert, perhaps *the* expert, on extraterrestrial life. When film director Stanley Kubrick and science fiction writer Arthur C. Clarke were working on the epoch-making science fiction film *2001: A Space Odyssey,* they called upon Carl Sagan to ask his opinion of what extraterrestrials might look like. Director Kubrick favored extraterrestrials that looked human. It was certainly a lot cheaper and easier to put some makeup on a bunch of actors, than to try to construct a profoundly alien-looking alien.

Sagan argued that it was highly unlikely that anything closely resembling a human being would evolve anywhere else in the Universe. On the other hand, constructed aliens would probably look phony: they usually do in science fiction films. Sagan suggested that the extraterrestrials not be shown explicitly at all, that the details of what they looked like be left to the viewer's imagination. Ultimately, after experimenting with a large number of possible extraterrestrial forms, Kubrick and Clarke decided that Sagan was right and settled on a completely surrealistic but very effective representation.

Actually, the general public has been far more eager to take the subject of extraterrestrial life seriously than has the bulk of the scientific community. Science fiction was widely read and it influenced the way many of us thought. Perhaps it influenced us a bit too much. During the 1950s and '60s a majority of the people in America believed, or half-believed, that we were being actively watched by extraterrestrials, who came to earth via round spaceships that were called flying saucers or UFOs. As a scientist, Sagan was not at all impressed by the purported evidence that UFOs were spaceships, but at least he was willing to discuss the subject publicly, and willing to speculate openly about the possibilities of life on other worlds, or a whole range of other fascinating but far-out topics. Sagan has been more than willing to discuss topics his more conservative and cautious colleagues won't touch.

Often the public at large regards scientists as a snobbish elite, unable or unwilling to talk to ordinary folks about what they are doing and thinking. All too often the public is quite correct in this perception. Many fine scientists simply lack the gift of communicating their ideas beyond a narrow circle of like-minded colleagues. Others lack the time or the interest. And there are those who sincerely believe that any sort of public acclaim will somehow compromise their position as serious scientists. They feel that the scientist who gets his name into the newspapers or is interviewed on television is "grandstanding."

Such views are utterly alien to Carl Sagan, who loves communicating science almost as much as he loves doing science. He believes passionately that a broad public understanding of science is not merely useful, but absolutely necessary in the modern world so dominated by science and technology. Modern scientific research is enormously expensive and much of it could not be carried out without public understanding and support. The public must be willing to pay, with tax dollars, for probes of other planets or radio-telescope explorations of distant stars.

Even more important, Sagan feels that the world itself may not survive, unless the public—you and I—understand science and its implications. Would the world's people continue to allow their leaders to prepare for nuclear war if they really knew what would happen as the result of such a war?

In addition to getting the information across clearly so that nonscientists can understand it, Sagan has also been able to communicate the excitement and sheer joy of the scientific quest. Isaac Asimov, no mean communicator of science himself, has said that Sagan has "the Midas Touch. Any subject he deals with turns to gold." A craftsman can communicate the basic facts clearly; it takes an artist, and yes, an entertainer, to have his audience share the emotion and the excitement.

Though for convenience Sagan is usually described as an astronomer and it is in this field—especially exploring the planets with spacecraft—that he has done most of his scientific work, his interests and training are wide-ranging. If a major science and public policy issue like the proposed Star Wars defense system comes up, Sagan is there, delivering his views through popular articles and on a host of TV interview shows. He is an astronomer who won his Pulitzer Prize writing about the evolution of human intelligence. He is a scientist who has written a best-selling work of science fiction. He is truly what writer Robert F. Moss called him, "The Scientist Superstar."

Our society today is in love with "superstars" from sports, the movies, television, music, even politics. Sagan is the only one from science. His position is utterly unique.

CHAPTER ONE

"But How Will You Make a Living?"

A major turning point in young Carl Sagan's life came in his sophomore year at Rahway High School in New Jersey. His biology teacher told him he was pretty sure that some people got paid for being astronomers. Up to that point Carl had assumed that he was going to have to work at some sort of regular job and pursue his interest in astronomy as a sideline. That worried him because he figured that he wasn't going to make a very good door-to-door salesman.

"What do you want to be when you grow up?" his grandfather had once asked him.

"An astronomer," he said.

"Yes," his grandfather replied quite reasonably, "but how will you make a living?"

In the world into which Carl Sagan was born people didn't become astronomers. In fact, people had only the foggiest notion of what an astronomer did, and no notion at all that one could not only make a living as an astronomer, but become rich and famous in the bargain.

Carl Edward Sagan was born on November 9, 1934, in the Bensonhurst section of Brooklyn. His father, Samuel, was a garment cutter who had been born in Russia but had come to the United States without his parents when he was five years old. His mother, Rachel, had been born in the U.S. The year 1934 was the middle of the Depression and Sagan remembers his family—he, his parents, and his younger sister, Cari—as "kind of poor."

There was nothing particularly unusual about Carl's childhood. He played stickball and did all of the other things that city kids of his age did. But he had one peculiarity. He was fascinated by the stars—you could still see the stars clearly at night in Bensonhurst in those days.

The sun and the moon, he recalls, seemed perfectly all right for Brooklyn, but the stars were different, somehow stranger and more interesting. When he asked people what the stars were, he usually got answers like, "They're lights in the sky, kid."

"I could tell they were lights in the sky, that wasn't what I meant."

When he was old enough to get a library card

Carl made an expedition to the nearest Brooklyn Public Library branch. "I had to take the streetcar; it was some big distance away." The first thing he asked for was a book on the stars and was promptly given a book on Hollywood stars. After all, what other kind of stars were kids of his age *supposed* to be interested in? At first he was too embarrassed to tell the librarian what sort of stars he really wanted to know about. But after a while the confusion was straightened out and he did get a book about those lights in the sky.

Carl devoured the book without ever leaving the library. It was a revelation to him because it said that the stars were like the sun except much, much farther away. The boy wasn't sure how far, but he thought about how bright the sun was and how dim the stars seemed, and he knew that they would have to be very, very far away indeed. "The scale of the Universe opened up for me."

A year or so later he learned about the planets, and how they revolved around the sun, and he figured that if the stars were like the sun, then they too must have planets revolving around them. This was not, Sagan noted, an original idea; astronomers had been speculating about planets revolving around other stars since the seventeenth century. But it was a new and absolutely original idea to eight-year-old Carl Edward Sagan. At that point, he says, he got very interested in astronomy. He also decided that the Universe was "full up," that there was life on many other planets revolving around other suns.

When he was about ten and attending P.S. 101 in Brooklyn, Carl discovered an entirely different type of book, the novels of Edgar Rice Burroughs. Burroughs is best known for his Tarzan stories, but he was a very prolific writer and the stories that most captivated young Sagan were the tales of John Carter, the gentleman adventurer from Virginia who had traveled in a spaceship to the planet Mars, or Barsoom, as Mars was known to its inhabitants.

The Burroughs tales were wildly romantic and they fired the boy's imagination. "I followed herds of eight-legged beasts of burden, the thoats. I won the hand of the lovely Dejah Thoris, Princess of Helium. I befriended a four-meter-high green fighting man named Tars Tarkas. I wandered within the spired cities and domed pumping stations of Barsoom, and along the verdant banks of the Nilosyrits and Nepenthes canals."

And so the fantasy Mars of Edgar Rice Burroughs deepened the young man's fascination with the possibility of life on other worlds.

Yet Carl was not entirely swept up in Burroughs' romantic vision. Edgar Rice Burroughs had a completely unfettered imagination; he cared nothing at all for the facts and his Mars in no way resembled the real Mars as Carl knew it, and increasingly this bothered him. "Slowly doubts began to gnaw."

A mainspring of the plot in one of the John Carter stories was based on the hero forgetting that the Martian year is longer than the earthly year. Yet it seemed elementary to Carl that the first thing anyone would do on going to Mars was check on how long the year was, and the day too. "I can recall no mention by Carter of the remarkable fact that the Martian day is almost [the same length] as the terrestrial day. It was as if he expected the familiar features of his home planet somewhere else." In some ways Burroughs had too little imagination and certainly too little knowledge.

The stories contained things which at first glance seemed startling, but on further reflection turned out to be disappointing. Sagan remembers that there were supposed to be two more primary colors on Mars than on Earth. He closed his eyes trying to imagine another primary color, but he couldn't come up with anything more original than a murky brown or plum. What was a primary color anyway? Finally he decided that Burroughs didn't entirely know what he was talking about. But still there was all that rousing adventure. "More than enough to maintain the interest of a city-bound ten-year-old in a Brooklyn summer."

That fall he chanced upon a copy of *Astounding Science Fiction* on the newsstand at the local candy store. *Astounding Science Fiction* was one of the better science fiction magazines of the day. It was a step or two above the sort of "space opera" written by

Burroughs. If the adventure wasn't quite as rousing, the science was certainly a lot better. Carl scraped together enough money to buy the magazine, carried his new treasure to a bench outside the store, sat down and read his first "modern" science fiction story.

It was a tale about time travel and nuclear war. Carl had heard about the atomic bombs which had recently been dropped on the Japanese cities of Hiroshima and Nagasaki, though he really wasn't sure how the bombs worked. Reading the story made him realize, for the first time, the enormous implications of the atomic bomb. It gave humanity the power to destroy the world. That was a startling, frightening realization and one that has continued to haunt him.

The time travel part of the story was intriguing, but frustrating. How could it be done? If the author knew, he certainly wasn't telling.

Carl eagerly read each new issue of *Astounding Science Fiction* and lots of other science fiction magazines as well. He began making scorecards for the stories, and found that most of them ranked very high in raising interesting questions, but they were not nearly as good in answering those questions. There were lots of other intellectual influences on young Carl Sagan's life—the writings of Bertrand Russell and Tom Paine, for example. They may have been more important than science fiction. But science fiction was first.

The end of World War II brought modest prosperity to the Sagan family. Samuel Sagan had risen from garment cutter to factory manager. The family followed the American dream of moving from the crowded city to the suburbs, in this case Rahway, New Jersey, across the Hudson River from New York City and farther south.

By this time Carl's academic and intellectual talents had been recognized, and it was then that the biology teacher told him that he really could think about making a living as an astronomer. As a top student, Carl assumed that he would have his choice of colleges, but which one to pick? He got a recruiting booklet from the University of Chicago, and printed on the cover were the words, "If You Want an Education."

Inside was a picture of a football game with the information that if you wanted to go to a school with a good football team, then you shouldn't pick the University of Chicago because the U. of C. didn't have a football team anymore.

There was another picture of a beer blast, along with the sobering caption that if you wanted a school with an active fraternity life, then you had better look elsewhere because fraternities at the U. of C. had been radically deemphasized.

"But," it said, "if you want an education, come to the University of Chicago." Said Sagan, "It sounded like the place for me."

It wasn't just that the University didn't have football or fraternities. "They indicated that education was their prime focus—education that was at once broad and deep. None of the other schools seemed to stress that."

Chicago had a splendid astronomy department. However, there was a problem. Among the things that the University of Chicago didn't have was an engineering school, and Sagan wanted to study engineering as well as astronomy. He wasn't particularly interested in engineering *per se,* but he was still under the influence of those early science fiction stories. To explore the planets you had to visit them. Lyman Spitzer, the well-known Princeton astronomer, finally assured the young man that you didn't really have to build a spaceship yourself in order to be a successful astronomer. There were plenty of other ways to study the stars and planets and others would build spaceships. Still, that early desire to actually get into a spaceship and visit other planets has never quite left him.

Sagan entered the University of Chicago at age sixteen in the fall of 1951. At that time the University was unique among American universities. Its chancellor was educational reformer Robert M. Hutchins, who had boldly attacked those two pillars of American college life, football and fraternities, and made education, not social life or job training, the central goal of the University.

The U. of C. was already an established center for science. On the faculty were such professors as Nobel Prize-winning chemist Harold Urey and Nobel Prize-winning physicist Enrico Fermi. Both had been among the key scientists in the secret Manhattan Project which had developed the atomic bomb during World War II. In fact, the first man-made, self-sustaining chain reaction—a crucial step in the development of the bomb, and all atomic energy—took place in a lab set up in the field house of the unused University of Chicago football stadium.

The U. of C. was also strong in the humanities, which Sagan liked. In an era of campus quiet and conformity the University was, in Sagan's words, "a very exciting place to be."

The world of this bright and ambitious young man was expanding rapidly. Back home in Rahway for Christmas vacation, Sagan met another student, a biologist, who was a friend of the family. The biologist was at the University of Indiana working under Nobel Prize-winner H. J. Muller. The biologist told Sagan that Muller was interested in the problem of the origin of life. Having taken major steps in expanding our knowledge of the nature of life on Earth, Muller's interests had naturally expanded to the origin of life and its cosmic distribution. That was the sort of big, basic problem that fascinated Sagan. When he got back to Chicago, Sagan wrote to his biologist friend in Indiana. The friend showed the letter to Muller, who became interested in the precocious young astronomer and invited Sagan to spend the summer of his freshman year working in his biology laboratory in Indiana.

This was to be Sagan's first real taste of scientific research, and he discovered that much of it is hard, routine labor. That summer Sagan spent most of his time breeding fruit flies in milk bottles, and checking to see what variations crossbreeding produced. The variations are generally small and predictable. Though work of this type is a basic and necessary part of genetic research, it isn't very exciting or glamorous.

There was, however, one memorable break in the routine. Sagan was checking a newly hatched batch of fruit flies when he found a specimen that didn't fit any of the expected patterns. The difference between this specimen and the other fruit flies in the batch was so startling that Sagan immediately concluded a major evolutionary change had taken place before his very eyes. However, the odds against a major evolutionary change happening in the laboratory are astronomical, and the young man wasn't quite sure how he was going to break this remarkable news to his famous boss.

As the young assistant was haltingly telling the renowned biologist what had happened, Muller stopped him, and then accurately described the new creature, without ever having seen it. Sagan was amazed. It was, Muller said, an old story, and the young man had made a common mistake. There was a kind of tiny moth that had adapted to life in genetics laboratories. The fruit flies were bred in sealed milk bottles. The moth didn't have anything to do with fruit flies, it just laid its eggs in the sticky mixture at the bottom of the milk bottles in which the flies also deposited their eggs. In the brief time that the bottles were unstoppered a moth could make a dive for the bottle, deposit its eggs, and escape unseen. Novice lab workers had been astonished and misled when they first found this tiny moth among the fruit flies. Sagan realized that he had not stumbled upon an evolutionary leap, "but [on] another lively adaptation in nature, itself the product of microevolution and natural selection."

Muller told Sagan that if he was interested in life on other worlds, then he had better learn biology and chemistry as well as astronomy. When he went back to the University of Chicago, Sagan carried with him a letter from Muller introducing him to Harold Urey, the world-famous chemist who was also doing work on the origin of life. Sagan recalls that Urey was a very kindly man. "I did an honors essay on how life began. It was very naîve, and I remember Urey's comment: 'This is the work of a very young man.' "

Sagan was certainly beginning to attract the attention of senior faculty members—not all of it favorable. Even at this early stage of his career he displayed gifts as a popularizer of science by organizing a campus lecture series on science, and including himself as one of the speakers. One faculty member derisively referred to the series as "Sagan's circus," but it filled the lecture hall regularly. Many scientists are suspicious of any popularization of science, even if it is done well.

Sagan has a restless and expansive imagination, and some have accused him of lacking the patience to do the hard slogging that is usually necessary in basic scientific research. This frequently repeated charge is one that Sagan vigorously denies. He points out that a lot of his scientific work has been the result of years of difficult and often tedious research. This sort of work is not visible to the general public.

Perhaps it is Sagan's ability to see the broader picture, and not get bogged down in detail, that makes some believe that he doesn't pay enough attention to detail. Sagan can also adjust quickly when presented with new information, rather than becoming completely wedded to one particular theory or interpretation. Ultimately these qualities have given him an enormous advantage as a popularizer of science. In a cover story on Sagan, *Time* magazine quotes one scientist: "Sagan can separate the momentous from the minute. He can tell the story without cluttering detail."

Sagan took a master's degree in physics from Chicago and then went on for a graduate degree in astronomy at Chicago's graduate school which was located in Williams Bay, Wisconsin. There he studied under Dutch astronomer Gerard Kuiper, one of only two full-time planetary astronomers in the United States at the time. Kuiper had made a number of extremely important astronomical discoveries; for example, he discovered new moons of Uranus and Neptune, and played a major role in the first U.S. unmanned exploration of the moon, the Ranger program. But Kuiper also had an interest in the possibility of life on other planets. He was one of the few astronomers in the world who was seriously and admittedly interested in this attention-grabbing topic.

The idea that there might be life on other planets, particularly Mars, had been popular around the turn of the century, but it had very much fallen out of scientific favor and by the 1950s it was barely respectable at all. Kuiper, an eminently respected and respectable scientist, was one of those helping to bring the search for life on other planets back into the scientific mainstream.

During the summer of 1956, Sagan went with Kuiper to the McDonald Observatory in Fort Davis, Texas. That summer turned out to be a major disappointment. Sagan spent a frustrating couple of months trying to look at Mars through the observatory's eighty-two-inch telescope. Says Sagan, "As it turned out there were dust storms in both places—Mars and Texas." Even under the best of conditions, Earth-based observations of the planets were going to be severely limited in value, for the observer was "sitting under a blanket of air forty million miles from the target." "That," Sagan commented, "was not going to tell me much."

While Sagan was studying for his doctorate under Kuiper, he met and married a young biologist named Lynn Alexander. The couple moved from Williams Bay to the pleasant university town of Madison, Wisconsin. (The Sagans were divorced in 1963. She is now a professor at Boston University.)

At this point Sagan came to the attention of the geneticist and recent Nobel Prize-winner Joshua Lederberg, who was to become a tremendous influence on the development of his ideas and the direction of his career. Lederberg had a formidable and fearsome reputation among graduate students. He was known to be a man both aloof and caustic, yet one day out of the blue, he called Carl Sagan and said that he wanted to discuss the subject of extraterrestrial life. In Lederberg, Sagan found a mind as bold and unfettered as his own. He came to regard Lederberg as his mentor and his friend.

Says Lederberg, "Back in the early days of our friendship I think it was helpful to Sagan that an established biologist could entertain the same thoughts as he did about extraterrestrial life."

In 1959 the National Academy of Sciences set up a special committee to study possible ways of searching for life in space. Lederberg was chairman of the committee and he asked the twenty-five-year-old Carl Sagan to be a member. The formation of that committee marked a major step in making the search for extraterrestrial life scientifically respectable again. If the National Academy of Sciences was interested, then it wasn't just science fiction anymore.

In the following year Sagan received his doctorate in astronomy and astrophysics from the University of Chicago. Now well-respected and well-connected, Sagan began to move smoothly from one prestigious academic position to another. Lederberg had gone to Stanford Medical School in California and he invited his young friend and colleague Carl Sagan to spend a year at Stanford as a visiting assistant professor of genetics. Sagan then moved on to the Smithsonian Astrophysical Observatory in Cambridge, Massachusetts, and to Harvard University where he held posts as both astrophysicist and assistant professor of astronomy.

In science, success is often measured by the number of papers a scientist has published. The general public often has difficulty understanding what this means. The scientific paper is the result of the scientist's work. He is putting a detailed account of the work before his scientific colleagues and saying, "Here is what I have done, and what I have concluded. What do you think?" In those early years Sagan's output of papers was prodigious. With Lederberg and other colleagues, he turned out scores of scientific papers in just a few years. A unifying theme for most of this work was physics and chemistry of the planets and the possibility of finding life beyond the Earth. So when the search for life in space began in earnest, Carl Sagan was uniquely qualified to become one of the leaders.

Not bad for a kid from Brooklyn who once thought he might have to become a door-to-door salesman in order to support his astronomy habit.

CHAPTER TWO

Interstellar and International Concerns

What is the daily life of a scientist like? If he is an astronomer, does he spend his time looking through telescopes or examining photographs of the stars and planets? Are hours consumed at the blackboard or computer terminal doing calculations? As a professor does he spend long periods of time preparing and delivering lectures to his students in the classroom, or working with a select group of graduate students? The answer to these questions is yes, of course. But there is much more to the life of a scientist than the laboratory and the classroom.

Many of us carry in the back of our minds an image of a scientist, perhaps drawn from old movies. He (almost all stereotypical scientists are male) is a white-coated eccentric who works obsessively and alone in some isolated laboratory for years until one day he bursts forth with an astounding and completely unexpected discovery. Or there is the "absent-minded professor," the fellow with the Albert Einstein haircut and chalk on his coat, who is so absorbed in his abstruse studies that he is barely aware of the practical world around him.

There may be some isolated scientists; there are certainly many abstracted and absent-minded ones. But to a degree larger than most nonscientists imagine, modern science is a very social and cooperative affair. Professors work with their graduate students, as well as with their colleagues. Much scientific work is done in teams. There are hundreds, perhaps thousands, of scientific organizations which hold what seem like an endless round of meetings and conferences—regional, national, and international. Then there are the scientific journals which are generally read by all scientists working within a particular discipline. There is private correspondence, there are phone calls, and personal meetings.

Ultimately a scientific discovery may take place within the brain of an individual scientist—but in reality no advance occurs in isolation; it is a result of almost constant communication with others who are working on and thinking about the same sort of problems. Scientists cooperate but they also compete over whose ideas are to be accepted, whose projects are to be pursued.

Scientists are often accused of living in an "ivory tower," that is, being isolated from many of the day-to-day concerns of ordinary folk. It's true that some scientists are by nature reclusive, and others so deeply involved in their own work that they have little contact with people outside of their own field. But the same can be said of some people in almost any profession.

Practically speaking, modern science is too important, and too expensive, to allow scientists the luxury of being uninvolved in the concerns of the outside world. Unlike Edgar Rice Burroughs' fictional John Carter, or the "gentlemen scientists" of an earlier era, most of today's scientists must work within the structure of a university, the government, or some other large institution. They are often courted by, or must court, government and private industry for research funds if nothing else.

At least since the development of the atomic bomb in 1945, science has become a dominant force in world politics, and the use or misuse of scientific discoveries has enormous practical and moral implications for every one of us.

So it's nearly impossible for any scientist to remain isolated and uninvolved, even if he or she desired it. And there is no indication that Carl Sagan has ever desired to remain uninvolved.

For his entire adult life Sagan has been in an academic world. After Harvard, he moved on to Cornell University at Ithaca, New York, where he not only became a professor of astronomy but director of the Laboratory for Planetary Studies, a very prestigious post for so young a man. In addition, he has been on a staggering number of government and professional boards and committees, mainly concerned with astronomy or space travel or the search for extraterrestrial life, but also biology, politics, even literature. He played a leading role in the *Mariner, Viking,* and *Voyager* expeditions to the planets, for which he received the NASA Medal for Exceptional Scientific Achievement; the Prix Galabert, the international astronautics prize; the NASA Medal for Distinguished Public Service (twice); and the John F. Kennedy Astronautics Award of the American Astronautical Society. His listing in *Who's Who* is almost a full column long and includes lectureships, prizes, advisory posts, and a dozen honorary degrees.

To give you an idea of the enormous scope of Sagan's activities, here is a small (a very small) sampling of some of the advisory groups and organizations to which he belongs or has belonged.

Chairman, Lander Imaging Flight Team Science Analysis Group, Project *Viking,* Jet Propulsion Laboratory.

Member, Executive Committee, Workshop on Extraterrestrial Intelligence, Ames Research Center, NASA.

Fellow, Committee for the Scientific Investigation of Claims of the Paranormal.

Chairman, Study Group on Machine Intelligence and Robotics, NASA headquarters.

Judge, National Book Awards.

Member, Steering Committee, Center on the Long-term Consequences of Nuclear War.

He is a member or fellow of societies as diverse as the American Astronomical Society, The American Physical Society, the Society for the Study of Evolution, The American Academy of Arts and Sciences, and The Explorer's Club.

Carl Sagan has been a prolific writer of both scientific and popular works, but he has also been an editor of both scientific and popular publications. For twelve years he was editor-in-chief of the journal *Icarus,* the leading professional journal devoted to planetary research. *Icarus* isn't the sort of magazine that you're likely to find at your local newsstand. But Sagan has also been a long-time contributing editor of the popular Sunday supplement magazine *Parade,* which your family probably gets along with its Sunday paper.

As noted, this is only a small sampling of committees, societies, and publications with which Sagan has been associated. Some of these positions are honorary, or nearly so, requiring little work. But more often than not, Sagan is actively involved, in meetings, in writing and speaking, as well as in reading and listening to the ideas of others. In short, Carl Sagan has been an extremely busy fellow. There has been no ivory tower, no hermit scientist's life for him.

Anyone who has ever seen Sagan on television, or read any of his popular books, knows that he is extremely bright and very, very articulate. He's not dogmatic, but he does hold definite opinions, and he is not at all shy or diffident about expressing them. Sometimes his outspokenness, and the sheer force of his personality, are not appreciated by his colleagues, particularly if they happen to be on a different side of a scientific argument.

During the 1960s and '70s, Sagan was on a number of scientific committees that were involved with planning landings on the moon and Mars. Unlike many other scientists and technicians, Sagan was never enthusiastic about manned landings on the moon. He had always believed that at our level of technical development robots could do scientific exploration of space more efficiently, cheaply, and safely than a human crew. Sagan was not the only scientist to hold this view; many, perhaps the majority, of professional astronomers would have agreed with him. But all of the objections to manned flight were swept away by the great national enthusiasm to put a man on the moon by the end of the 1960s, which Sagan stresses was done mainly for political, not for scientific purposes.

One of the underlying themes in Carl Sagan's thinking is that there might be an abundance of different forms of life in space. Studying alien lifeforms, Sagan believes, is the only way to develop a broad understanding of biology—all life on Earth is chemically the same because it all has evolved from a single instance of the origin of life. Biologists don't know what other kinds of life are possible. Once again it must be emphasized that Sagan was not alone in his expansive view about the possibilities of life, but as usual he was a spokesman and a leader. The theories and possibilities he presented showed a fine imaginative mind at work, but they also raised a host of practical problems for those who were designing the space probes. Sagan suggested that microbes might, just might, exist beneath the surface of the moon! Most scientists were quite convinced that the moon was biologically barren, but Sagan was able to marshal a scientifically credible argument for the possibility of microbes on the moon. He didn't say it was likely, but he argued that the possibility was too important to ignore.

At one time this was the sort of subject that scientists could argue happily about in conferences and in articles and letters to their journals. But in the 1960s the U.S. was actually planning to send men to the moon, and these men were going to bring back samples of lunar rocks and dust. What had once been a theoretical argument now raised a host of nagging concerns for the scientists and technicians of NASA.

If one admitted the possibility, however small, of lunar microbes, then one confronts the possibility, tiny but still there, that some of these theoretical microbes might be dangerous, even deadly to human beings. If such microbes were brought back to Earth they might introduce some sort of completely unknown "super germ" to our planet, with horrifying results. Now if all this sounds a lot like science fiction to you, you are not alone. A lot of scientists regarded such fears as exactly that. In fact, the germs from space theme has cropped up in many science fiction tales. But still Sagan's arguments and those of like-minded scientists carried enough weight for NASA planners to require a quarantine on material brought back from the moon.

The public was puzzled by the quarantine because most people had simply assumed that the moon was a "dead world." Some scientists, particularly geologists, were angry because the quarantine, which they felt didn't work very effectively anyway, was making their study of the lunar rocks much more difficult.

After five moon landings, when practically everyone else was convinced that there were no microbes on the moon, Sagan was still saying they might be there, if one dug deep enough to look for them. Sagan's arguments were ingenious and he was persistent. And what if he had been correct?

There was another side to the contamination coin. Perhaps Earth might not be contaminated by germs from the moon or Mars, but microbes from our space probes might contaminate Mars.

So what? you say. Well, germs from Earth might

injure or even wipe out any life on the planet. This was also a theme in science fiction going all the way back to H. G. Wells. Less dramatic, but more likely for those scientists like Sagan, who were deeply interested in the possibilities of finding life on Mars, was that earthly microbes might confuse and deceive those looking for life. What if microbes were found on Mars. They might originally have been stowaways from Earth on Mars probes, like rats aboard an explorer's ship being brought to a newly discovered island. Then how would you know what Martian bugs were like?

Most scientists agreed that any probe of another planet should be sterilized to avoid contaminating that planet. But Sagan went even further. He was one of those who argued that the craft that were designed to orbit Mars but not land should also be throughly sterilized, because eventually they would crash onto the Martian surface. Some of Sagan's colleagues felt that once again he was going too far and needlessly raising time-consuming problems for technicians.

At stake in keeping other planets free from contamination was not only a chance to see what life might be like on other worlds, but a chance to look at how life itself might have first developed. If a planet were contaminated that chance might be irrevocably lost. Sagan's commitment to keeping other planets uncontaminated was and is a passionate one.

Many of those meetings and conferences that Sagan has attended are with scientists from the Soviet Union or other nations that are considered political adversaries of the United States. The U.S. and USSR are the two leading space powers. Scientific discoveries have often been used for nationalistic purposes, but science itself is international, and scientists are as close to an international community as we have in the world today. Another of Sagan's passions is to preserve science as a truly international effort. The exploration of space, indeed any scientific endeavor, should ideally help to bring the world together, not blow it apart. But often governments will not allow this, and insist on treating science as part of foreign policy, even espionage.

In his early book, *The Cosmic Connection,* Sagan describes an incident when he was doing postdoctoral work at the University of California, when his strong interest in the exploration of space and the sterilization of space vehicles was well known.

One morning he got a call from an Air Force general he had met at several conferences. The general said that he was at the Los Angeles airport with some Soviet scientists, one of whom was an important figure in the Soviet effort to detect life on other planets. The general asked if Sagan would be interested in meeting the Soviets. Sagan jumped at the chance and rushed to the airport to catch a plane to Los Angeles.

When he arrived at the Los Angeles address that

the general had given him, Sagan found that there were a couple of other American scientists as well as three Soviets. There was also a translator whom Sagan calls Igor Rogovin, though that was not his name. Rogovin had been assigned to translate for the Russians during their visit. This struck Sagan as odd, since all three Russians spoke quite good English. Still, Rogovin was always busy. There was no conversation that he was not a part of. Sagan describes him acting like "a manic bee obsessively flitting from flower to flower."

At one point the whole group was to go out to dinner, and they could not all fit into one car. Sagan found himself in a car with the Soviet space scientist. Rogovin and the others were in a second car. During the half hour or so drive, Sagan and the Russian talked about methods of life detection and space vehicle sterilization. It was the first such contact the young Sagan ever had with a Soviet scientist.

Before dinner Sagan found himself alone with Igor Rogovin, who said to him in the tones of a Hollywood private eye, "Hey kid, what'd ya find out?"

Sagan, who described himself at that period of his life as "unwise in the ways of the world," was very pleased with the fruitful discussion he just had with the Russian and told Rogovin all about it.

"Pretty good, kid," said Rogovin. "Who do you work for?"

Sagan said the University of California.

"No, kid, not the cover."

Suddenly Sagan realized what was going on. This translator was really an American intelligence agent trying to glean bits and pieces of information from the Soviet scientists, and he thought that Sagan was one too.

At dinner Sagan found himself seated next to the Soviet space scientist. They talked about movies and poetry, just about anything but science. "I found myself unable to talk to him on any subject remotely approaching science." Any possibility of a useful exchange had been effectively killed by someone's attempt to turn the meeting into an intelligence-gathering opportunity.

The next day an enraged Carl Sagan called the Central Intelligence Agency to complain. Naturally he assumed that the CIA was responsible for Igor Rogovin. The CIA seemed genuinely concerned by what he told them. After an investigation the Agency informed Sagan that Rogovin didn't work for them, but was in fact an employee of Air Force Intelligence. No CIA agent, he was assured, would behave so foolishly.

A couple of years later at an international meeting of space scientists in Italy, Sagan once again met the Soviet scientist he had seen in Los Angeles. Following behind him at a discreet distance and now sporting a beard was Igor Rogovin. The Russian leaned over to Sagan and said, "Isn't that the fellow who was with us in Los Angeles?" Sagan said that it was. "Very stupid fellow," said the Russian.

"There are many other such stories involving both American and Soviet intelligence organizations," Sagan writes. "The general effect of such incidents is to detract from the credibility of legitimate scientific exchanges among scientists of different countries." In Sagan's view the fact that the Soviets regularly engage in the same sort of activity still doesn't make the intrusion of "intelligence" activities into international scientific exchanges right or "intelligent."

In 1966 Sagan took part in an outstanding and unusual example of international cooperation. In collaboration with a Soviet scientist, the late I. S. Shklovskii, he produced a book called *Intelligent Life in the Universe.* The book was a milestone, a broad, ranging work of science and speculation.

It was only a semitechnical book and made a lot of nonscientists realize that the possibility of intelligent life elsewhere in the Universe was not necessarily crazy or "unscientific," that scientists, at least the free spirits among them, were willing to speculate on the topic. And a few of them both in the U.S. and the USSR were bold enough to share their speculations with the rest of us.

The collaboration of an American and Soviet scientist seemed unique back in 1966. Actually there had often been cooperation between American scientists and their Soviet counterparts, but people outside of the scientific community were rarely aware of it. So the book not only informed people about the possibilities of communicating with civilizations on other worlds, but also highlighted the possibilities of communicating with people in other nations on this planet.

Intelligent Life in the Universe attracted a good deal of attention, both because of the subject and because it was the joint product of an American and a Russian. It is still viewed as the classic work in the field. At the age of thirty-two, a tender age for a scientist, Carl Sagan was making a mark for himself. His concerns of that time, both in space and here on Earth, still dominate his thinking today.

CHAPTER THREE

Beyond the Solar System

One of Carl Sagan's projects will last longer than the pyramids. It will outlast any other current human artifact, and pessimists have commented that it may well outlast the human race itself. Nothing better illustrates Sagan's boldness and his knack of grabbing the public's interest and attention than the small golden plaque attached to the *Pioneer 10* spacecraft.

Pioneer 10 itself was a very bold project, conceived and carried out in the early 1970s. That was the enthusiastic heyday of scientific space research. The *Pioneer* craft was designed to explore the environment in the outer solar system, primarily the giant planet Jupiter. After the probe completed its primary mission and passed Jupiter, *Pioneer 10* would then be given a push by Jupiter's powerful gravity, and thrown beyond the outer planets to become the first man-made object ever to leave the solar system. It was a grand and extravagant gesture.

The space probe was not designed to send back any messages from beyond the solar system. Nor was it specifically aimed at the planetary system of any nearby star (if indeed any nearby star has a planetary system). *Pioneer 10* was to be cast off after completing its mission to travel silently in the vastness of interstellar space for hundreds of millions of years. It would become a derelict in space.

But what if this derelict space probe were to be encountered by an advanced extraterrestrial civilization? What would they make of it? The extraterrestrials would probably be able to recognize the probe as artifically constructed rather than a natural object. But they would have no way of knowing where *Pioneer* came from and they would know nothing of its makers.

When Sagan first heard that *Pioneer 10* was to leave the solar system, he conceived an ambitious plan. Why not put some sort of message aboard the craft so that any aliens who might encounter it would at least have some chance of answering basic questions about where it came from and who sent it?

Sagan immediately contacted the National Aeronautics and Space Administration (NASA). *Pioneer* had already been in the planning stages for a long time, and it was getting very late to make any alterations in the program. But much to Sagan's surprise and delight, everybody in the NASA hierarchy was enthusiastic. Everyone seemed to agree, "Why not try?" The usually protracted and painful process of making even tiny changes in a spacecraft plan was bypassed, and the message project was swiftly approved.

The next step was deciding what sort of message to send. How do you even attempt to communicate with a theoretical extraterrestrial intelligence about which you know absolutely nothing? Obviously the alien is unlikely to understand English or any other earthly language. The message, said Sagan, had to be written in the only language that could conceivably be universal, the language of science. Sagan felt that the message should, first and foremost, be intended to convey certain basic scientific principles, which should be known to all intelligent beings. This information would prove that the senders of the message were also intelligent. Sagan discussed various possible messages with his Cornell colleague, radio astronomer Frank Drake, during a meeting of the American Astronomical Society in December of 1971. The basic form of the message was drafted in just a few hours.

Says Sagan, "At top left is a schematic representation of the hyperfine transition between parallel and antiparallel proton and electron spins of the neutral hydrogen atom. Beneath this representation is the binary number 1. Such transitions of hydrogen are accompanied by the emission of a radio-frequency photon of wavelength about 21 centimeters and frequency of about 1,420 megahertz. Thus, there is a characteristic distance and a characteristic time associated with the transition. Since hydrogen is the most abundant atom in the galaxy, and physics is the same throughout the galaxy, we think there will be no difficulty for an advanced civilization to understand this part of the message."

It is embarrassing to realize that most of the people on this planet would be unable to understand that part of the message of *Pioneer 10.* Indeed, most people can't even understand the explanation! But Sagan and his associates believed, quite reasonably, that a civilization advanced enough to be able to capture the *Pioneer* craft in deep space would also contain some individuals who would be able to interpret this diagram.

Much of the rest of the message was concerned with trying to communicate when and where the craft had been launched. It attempts to show our solar system in relation to fourteen powerful pulsars, among the most prominent features of our galaxy.

"But pulsars are cosmic clocks that are running down at largely known rates. The recipients of the message must ask themselves not only where it was ever possible to see fourteen pulsars arrayed in such a relative position, but also *when* it was possible to see them. The answers are: Only from a very small volume of the Milky Way galaxy and in a single year in the history of the galaxy. Within that small volume there are perhaps a thousand stars; only one is anticipated to have the array of planets with relative distances indicated at the bottom of the diagram." That one is, of course, our own sun.

In addition to the schematic and scientific side of the message, it was decided to add an additional more human touch. So the message also included a drawing of two nude human figures, male and female. The drawings were made by Sagan's second wife, artist Linda Salzman. Ironically, extraterrestrials might be able to understand the schematics perfectly but might be completely puzzled by the drawings. On Earth, however, the meaning of the drawings was obvious, and they were destined to become the most familiar and, in a way, the most controversial part of the entire *Pioneer* message project.

The message was to be engraved on a 6-inch by 9-inch gold anodized aluminum plate, and attached to the antenna support of the spacecraft. Because the erosion rate in interstellar space is extremely small it is expected that the plate will remain readable for hundreds of millions of years or longer.

It took about three weeks from the time the idea was presented and approved for the message to be designed and engraved. That figure may, in its way, be as impressive as the length of time that the message plate is expected to endure. There may be no project in the history of the U.S. space program that was completed so quickly. NASA was so happy with the message that an identical plaque was put on *Pioneer 11* when it was launched in 1973.

Sagan's "message to the stars" grabbed public attention in the most extraordinary way. Representations of the plaque appeared in newspapers and magazines throughout the world. A few delicately airbrushed the nude figures, "A family newspaper must uphold community standards . . ." huffed one editor.

When the *Los Angeles Times* ran the plaque on the front page it received an indignant letter protesting "sexual exploitation" and complaining that the space agency had "found it necessary to spread this filth even beyond our own solar system."

However, such reactions were quite rare, and in general the nude drawings provoked no great moral outrage. Sagan was worried about the possibility of prudish resistance within NASA, but to his relief he encountered none.

One thing about the drawings that Sagan did feel rather badly about was that in our multiracial world the figures in the message looked distinctly white. It wasn't meant to be that way. "We had hoped to represent at least three of the major races of mankind." The woman was to be given a partially Asian appearance, but since her hair was drawn only in outline, she looks like a blonde. The man was given a broad nose, thick lips, and a short Afro haircut. Somewhere between the original sketch and the final engraving the short Afro was changed to a curly haircut. So the figures were not quite as representative of the diversity of the human race as Sagan had hoped that they would be.

There were other quibbles. Why did the man have his right hand raised? On Earth, Sagan said, this is a universal sign of peace. Then someone, perhaps not seriously, suggested that if the extraterrestrials had somehow picked up old war movies that had been broadcast on TV, they might think the man was giving the Nazi salute. Since the Nazis were shown as evil, the extraterrestrials might conclude that the message was from the "bad guys." (A faint echo of this fear turns up in Sagan's 1985 novel, *Contact.*) Some women complained that while the male figure was giving the greeting, the female figure wasn't doing anything, just standing there with her hands at her sides.

A few fearful folk wondered whether somehow this message might be betraying our presence to hostile extraterrestrials. Sagan doubted if this represented much of a danger. If we're trying to hide from other intelligences in the galaxy, he said, it may already be too late.

Sagan pointed out that radio signals have been leaking into space since the first broadcasts, and reaching significant intensity in the 1920s. The radio and, later, TV signals travel much more quickly than the *Pioneer* craft. An advanced technological civilization might just be able to pick up "the tinny transmissions of Enrico Caruso arias, the Scopes trial, the 1928 election returns, the big jazz bands." They could be watching Uncle Miltie, Howdy Doody, the Kennedy-Nixon debates, and MTV.

And perhaps they might see some of those old World War II films about the Nazis, so maybe that fear about misunderstanding the upraised right hand is not entirely in the realm of fantasy.

There were a few technical criticisms from the scientific community as well, but overall, scientists and nonscientists alike responded to this way-out project with tremendous enthusiasm. Sagan had managed to capture the imagination of a public that was already beginning to get bored with the space program. Suddenly the possibility of actually communicating with other intelligences became real and thinkable.

The chances of the message of the *Pioneer* probe actually reaching some beings that could make sense out of it are literally astronomical, as Sagan well knew. He referred to the project as "good fun." The real target of the message, he acknowledged, was not out among the stars, but back here on Earth. "The transmittal of the *Pioneer 10* message encourages us to consider ourselves in cosmic perspective."

Though the *Pioneer* message was the longest of

long shots, Sagan and NASA were pleased enough with it to place another even more ambitious message aboard another probe, *Voyager,* that would ultimately be bound for the depths of interstellar space. The primary aim of the two *Voyager* craft, like that of the *Pioneer* probes, was to send back information from the farther planets, Jupiter, Saturn, Uranus, and Neptune. The *Voyager* probes, however, were more sophisticated and could relay much more detailed information. It was assumed that the probes would probably stop transmitting after passing Saturn, but that the silent and derelict craft would continue on out of the solar system. *Voyager 2* confounded and delighted the experts, for early in 1986, the still-operating space probe sent back wonderful photographs and huge quantities of other data from near the planet Uranus, making it the most spectacularly successful planetary probe ever.

Since there was more time to plan for the *Voyager* probes, the message was far more complex and richer than the simple plaques on *Pioneer.* The information is contained on gold-plated copper phonograph records that should last a billion years. Also on the probes are a cartridge and stylus, so the record can be played, and on the aluminum record jacket are the instructions on how it can be played. The jacket also contains information on the position of the Earth, so the finders may know where it came from.

This time the bulk of the message was not to be

scientific information. Sagan and his coworkers figured that any civilization that could intercept *Voyager* in deep space would know a lot more about science than those sending the message did. The senders did not have to prove that they knew elementary science. That would be obvious from the fact that they were able to construct the craft in the first place.

The record contains other information that might interest extraterrestrials, information that is aimed at presenting its senders in the best possible light:

"Although the recipients may not know any languages of Earth, we included greetings in sixty human tongues, as well as the hellos of the humpback whales. We sent photographs of humans from all over the world caring for one another, learning, fabricating tools and art, and responding to challenges. There is an hour and a half of exquisite music from many cultures, some of it expressing our sense of cosmic loneliness, our wish to end our isolation . . ."

There is much more, including an attempt to send the thoughts and feelings of a single individual. The electrical activity of this person's brain, heart, eyes, and muscles were recorded for an hour. They were then transcribed into sound, compressed in time, and included on the record. "In one sense we have launched into the Cosmos a direct transcription of the thoughts and feelings of a single human being in the month of June in the year 1977."

The sheer audacity of the project is staggering. The chances of any sort of success at all is so slim that cynics might find the whole thing laughable. But Sagan has never been a cynic about the potential of life. "We have sent [the message] because it is important to try."

The *Voyager* project was to be very important to Carl Sagan personally as well. Creative director of the project was Ann Druyan, a novelist and television writer and a woman who shared Sagan's cosmic vision. It was during the *Voyager* project that the two, who had known each other for years, fell in love. Ann Druyan was to become Carl Sagan's third wife, and close coworker on many of his future projects. It was her brain waves that are encoded on the *Voyager* record.

The messages of *Pioneer* and *Voyager* are dramatic, and indeed it may be "important to try," as Sagan has said, but when it comes to really searching for intelligent life in the Universe then the "note in the bottle" tossed into the cosmic ocean approach is hardly the most efficient. The best approach, Sagan and most other astronomers contend, is to use radio signals.

As we said, human beings have already been sending radio and TV transmissions to the stars, quite accidentally for many years. And it is possible that there are some advanced civilizations out there somewhere with the technology to pick up and actually make some sense out of these faint and accidental messages. Can you image some alien out there puzzling over Howdy Doody?

If extraterrestrial intelligences might pick up an accidental radio transmission from Earth, then it is also possible that we might be able to pick up some radio transmission from other intelligent life in the Universe—especially if "they" are trying to communicate with us. This idea appealed strongly to Sagan's fellow extraterrestrial life enthusiast, Frank Drake. Drake had gathered together a small group of like-minded scientists, to see what might be done.

The first discussions of the project, which was to be called Ozma, after the ruler of the mythical land of Oz, were conducted so quietly that they were almost held in secret. The scientists involved were not afraid of revealing any secret information, for none was involved. It was just that at that time, the early 1970s, the idea of searching for extraterrestrial life was still considered both mildly disreputable and unscientifically sensational. The scientists feared that they would be criticized for wasting time and money on an "impossible" project, on the one hand, but on the other hand they might be overwhelmed by reporters and others who were deeply interested in what they were doing, but still did not understand what was involved. They were afraid that their project would be treated like science fiction.

In fact, Ozma, like *Pioneer,* was received surprisingly well by the general public. There was some sensationalizing but not much. Sagan can claim part of the credit for this good reception. Back in 1966, when the search for intelligent life in the Universe was still considered scientifically disreputable in some quarters, Sagan had teamed up with Soviet astrophysicist I. S. Shklovskii (a man with as expansive an imagination as Sagan's own) to write the book, *Intelligent Life in the Universe.* In it the two scientists boldly went where no man, certainly no reputable scientist, had gone for a long time. They went into a serious discussion of the possibilities of other intelligences existing in the Universe, as well as a far-ranging discussion of the possibilities of contacting them, or being contacted by them. The book helped to bring the subject of the search for extraterrestrial intelligence out of the dark ages of scientific disrepute.

Ozma didn't pick up any promising signals, and the project was not carried out for long. But it did not end in disgrace. It was recognized as a pioneering effort. Other radio astronomy projects have followed.

In November, 1974, Drake launched another effort, this time using the opposite tactic; instead of listening for signals, the astronomers tried to deliberately transmit powerful messages aimed at specially selected parts of the galaxy. The instrument used to beam these messages was the gigantic radio telescope at Arecibo, Puerto Rico. The Arecibo Observatory is run by Cornell University.

The Arecibo message, which contained basic scientific information, was aimed at the globular cluster known only as M13, which is about 25,000 light-years away. Even if the message reaches beings in M13 that can recognize it as having an intelligent origin, we won't know of our success for at least 50,000 years, which is the round-trip light travel time to M13. Even communication with a relatively nearby star could take hundreds of years.

Given the present state of our technology, we are probably better listeners than speakers, so projects aimed at picking up signals are deemed more practical. Few scientists anymore believe that organized searches for interstellar communication are a waste of time.

Characteristically, Carl Sagan favors the active approach. He realizes that the radio telescope search for extraterrestrial intelligence is not one that is likely to pay off quickly. Even in his most optimistic opinion it is a task that could take decades, or longer, but he concludes that the effort would be "sufficiently important for our view of the Universe and ourselves" to be worth it. The main obstacle to the search, he said back in 1973, is money. Radio astronomy is expensive and the project could cost tens of millions of dollars. That is a great deal of money, to be sure, but peanuts when compared to the cost of a single advanced weapons system.

Sagan has never given up on the idea of a radio search for signs of intelligent life. Despite the fact that funds for this sort of pure scientific research are harder than ever to come by, he has seen some success in the area. A project sponsored jointly by Harvard University and The Planetary Society, of which Sagan is president, is currently scanning an enormous range of radio signals from space, for signs of artificial origin. Hopefully, the National Aeronautics and Space Administration will soon begin an even more ambitious radio search project. Sagan has lobbied hard and effectively for both of these efforts. But he still feels there is a great deal more that could be done.

"A society," Sagan has said, "is measured not only by how it treats its people, but also by its great projects."

CHAPTER FOUR

UFOs and Dr. Velikovsky

It was inevitable that Carl Sagan and UFOs would collide. Anyone who was young during the late 1940s and early '50s would certainly have heard of UFOs. Actually, virtually everyone of any age has heard of UFOs and some people still "believe" in them in a vague sort of way. But during the late 1940s and early '50s an awful lot of people "believed" in UFOs, that is, believed that the Earth was being visited by spaceships from another world. UFOs, or flying saucers, were a very hot topic. Certainly a young man who had once been a regular reader of science fiction, who wanted to be an astronomer and had a passionate interest in the possibility of extraterrestrial life, would have had more than a passing interest in the many tales of extraterrestrial visitation that filled the air.

UFOs is one of those topics that most scientists like to stay as far away from as possible. When, in the late 1960s, the U.S. Air Force wanted to fund a scientific study of UFOs, they had trouble finding anyone in the scientific community who would touch the subject. The man who finally did head the study, the late Edward U. Condon, ultimately came to regret bitterly that he had ever gotten mixed up with UFOs, for he became embroiled in so much ugly and exhausting controversy.

But Sagan has never been one to shy away from controversy. Sagan's opinion of UFOs, that he doesn't "believe" in them, means he doesn't think there is any good evidence that the mysterious lights and objects that people have reported seeing in the sky are extraterrestrial spaceships.

Such an opinion might seem rather strange and narrow for the man who has speculated so freely and boldly on the possibilities of extraterrestrial life, the man who more than any other individual has given the search for intelligent life in the Universe scientific respectability. Sagan has frequently said that in the vastness of the Universe it is almost inconceivable to him that life has not developed elsewhere, probably in many, many places. Sagan's own writings about the possibility, indeed the likelihood of extraterrestrial civilizations, and his leadership in attempts to make contact with such civilizations had cheered many a die-hard UFO enthusiast. Sagan was the man who designed the messages to extraterrestrials put aboard the *Pioneer* and *Voyager* space probes.

If an earthly Carl Sagan believes in the possibility of contacting extraterrestrial civilizations, then why isn't he sympathetic to the idea of an extraterrestrial Carl Sagan trying to contact his earthly counterpart?

For years Sagan has been an outspoken nonbeliever in the extraterrestrial hypothesis for UFOs. To some UFO believers this makes Sagan not only a nonbeliever but a heretic. On his very first "Tonight" show appearance, in 1972, Johnny Carson asked Sagan about UFOs, and he responded in no uncertain terms. UFOs are always an attention grabber, and Sagan feels there is nothing wrong with grabbing the public's attention, so long as what you are telling them is accurate. He has characterized the continuing interest in UFOs as more a matter of faith than science.

Why this seemingly parochial view for so expansive a thinker? The reason is simple. Sagan, like virtually all of his scientific colleagues, is totally unimpressed by the evidence that UFOs are extraterrestrial. "The evidence is simply rotten," says Sagan. "The key point is that of the million UFO cases reported since 1947, there has not been a single incident where something was reliably reported by many different people and, at the same time, was so exotic that it could only be an extraterrestrial spacecraft. It is very easy to be fooled. Moreover, no one has secured a close-up photograph of a presumptive extraterrestrial UFO, a scraping from the hull, a page from the captain's logbook or the like. . . . No one would be happier than me if we were being visited by extraterrestrials, but we must demand only the most rigorous standards of evidence when the stakes are so high."

Beyond this is the sheer improbability of multiple visits from intelligent extraterrestrials over the last forty years. In Sagan's view this hypothesis is defeated by the vastness of space. The distances are so inconceivably huge that even if there are large numbers of advanced civilizations out there, the chance of them visiting us even once, much less regularly—as UFO supporters indicate—is, in every sense of the word, astronomical. Not completely impossible, mind you, but wildly improbable. To entertain such an improbable hypothesis one would need very good evidence, and it just isn't there.

But what if we expand the time limits. Let's say we abandon the idea of repeated visits over the last forty years or so, and imagine that extraterrestrials may have visited the Earth only once or twice over the last ten thousand years. This is the basis of what came to be known as the ancient astronaut theory. It's really an offshoot of belief in UFOs, but suggests that human civilization was the result of a contact between primitive humans and technologically advanced visitors from the stars. According to this theory, the myths of the gods from the sky, so common in ancient civilizations, were, in reality, dim reflections of a real extraterrestrial contact at the dawn of civilization.

The ancient astronaut theory was popularized in Erich Von Daniken's book, *Chariot of the Gods* (1970), an enormous international best seller. *Chariot of the Gods* was followed by a series of similar books by Von Daniken and others which generated public interest in the subject for years.

Ironically, Sagan had speculated on the possibility of ancient extraterrestrial contacts long before Von Daniken and the others wrote their best sellers. In the classic *Intelligent Life in the Universe,* which Sagan wrote with Soviet astrophysicist I. S. Shklovskii, the authors examined a very ancient Sumerian legend. This legend, said Sagan and Shklovskii, is "suggestive of contact between our ancestors and an apparent representative of a superior society." But as "suggestive" and "provocative" as Sagan and Shklovskii found this and other ancient legends, they also found that it was quite impossible to demonstrate extraterrestrial contact from this sort of material which was open to so many interpretations. "We concluded there was *no* evidence for past visits."

What about ancient drawings and other artifacts that appear to indicate contact? Sagan finds these even less persuasive than the legends. Why, he asks, should beings from other planets look just like our own astronauts right down to the space suits they wear? Why would they need airfields, and arrive in rockets? All this he finds "less credible than the idea of visitation itself." The people who promote such ideas do not have too much imagination, but too little.

The whole search for extraterrestrial visitors, ancient or modern, Sagan finds "unprofitable." If new evidence arises, Sagan is happy to examine it. But the evidence is so slight, the probability of finding anything so remote, that it just isn't worth wasting much time over, he believes.

Carl Sagan has emerged as one of the most prominent opponents of UFOs, yet unlike many other UFO debunkers, he has never sought simply to dismiss the subject as being beneath notice. He has actually tried to encourage public debate, even among scientists. In 1969 Sagan helped to organize a scientific symposium on UFOs. It was the first time in over a quarter century that both pro and anti-UFO spokesmen squared off in an open forum. A lot of scientists had been against holding such a meeting at all, fearing that any discussion in a respectable format would lend credibility to the UFO crazies. Some even tried to have the meeting canceled.

That sort of approach is foreign to Sagan, who has always believed in the widest possible public discussion of all issues relating to science. In the past, UFOs had been a topic that generated a great deal of heat, but the symposium turned out to be a relatively even-tempered affair. Each side, of course, was convinced that it had been a clear winner in the debate; however, it is significant to note that interest in UFOs has declined markedly over the last seventeen years. At the very least, those who believe that UFOs are extraterrestrial spaceships can no longer claim that they have never been given a fair hearing by the scientific community.

If scientists give even the appearance of attempting to suppress or censor open discussion of an unorthodox or unpopular idea, the results can be disastrous. Nothing in recent history shows this more clearly than what has been called the Velikovsky Affair.

Sagan's involvement with the Velikovsky Affair is even more significant than his involvement with UFOs, because this case seemed to strike at the very heart of the scientific method. What happened got a lot of very intelligent people wondering whether scientists had not become some sort of new high priesthood that jealously guarded its own prestige and its own version of the truth from any outside inquiry.

To understand why this rather curious incident became such a source of bitter controversy and misunderstanding it is necessary to know something of Dr. Immanuel Velikovsky and his theories. He is little more than a footnote in the history of science today, but back in the 1950s he was big news, and a big headache for scientists.

Velikovsky was a Russian-born psychoanalyst and

scholar. He had been trained in a variety of disciplines at some of the best universities in Europe, and had come to the United States to escape the Nazis. He was a highly educated, extremely intelligent, very scholarly man who numbered among his acquaintances another escapee from Nazi persecution, Albert Einstein. Though Velikovsky had studied some science, he was not in any sense a trained scientist, particularly in areas such as astronomy and geology.

Velikovsky did not begin with an attempt to challenge orthodox science and history. He really began by trying to prove that the miraculous events described in the Old Testament were quite literally true and could be explained scientifically. In order to do this he had to explain, for example, how the Red Sea could be parted, how Joshua was able to make the sun appear to stand still in the sky, where the manna from Heaven came from, what was the source of the plagues of Egypt, and so on.

Velikovsky concluded that during the period of the Exodus the Earth had undergone an unprecedented series of catastrophes which could account for the apparent "miracles." Velikovsky then retired to the library at Columbia University for nine years researching his theories. His researches took him not only into astronomy and geology but into biology and history as well. The deeper he probed, the more expansive his theory became and the more established theories it challenged.

Briefly, Velikovsky's theory was this: A gigantic comet erupted from the planet Jupiter and passed by Earth around 1500 B.C. This near-miss stopped or slowed the planet, causing all manner of cataclysmic upheavals—the parting of the Red Sea, for example. The comet passed again fifty-two years later, creating another series of worldwide cataclysms. Still later the comet had an encounter with the planet Mars, which "tamed" the comet's flight and transformed it into what we now know as the planet Venus. However, Mars was roaming the solar system and passed close to Earth on several occasions during the eighth century B.C., initiating a new series of lesser but still enormous upheavals.

This summary hardly does justice to Velikovsky's proposals, which were extremely complex and far-ranging. In the beginning he relied primarily on the Old Testament and the records of other ancient civilizations to back up his claims. But he also said that he found evidence for his ideas in astronomy, geology, and physics as well.

Velikovsky put his ideas into a book called *Worlds in Collision.* Before the book was published in 1950 its contents were enthusiastically previewed in *Harper's* magazine, a nonscientific but highly respected publication.

The scientific community's reaction to the theories of Immanuel Velikovsky was one of amazement. His ideas seemed so at variance with well-established facts, his methods of research so lacking in any semblance of scientific discipline that scientists could not understand how any intelligent person could take him seriously. When the scientists discovered that a lot of intelligent nonscientists did take Velikovsky very seriously indeed, they were shocked. When scientists attacked Velikovsky and his theories they did it in the worst possible way.

Some of the early critics of Velikovsky were careless and they had underestimated his skills and tenacity. Velikovsky seized upon the errors of his critics, minor though they may have been, and used them to discredit all criticism of his theories.

Worst of all, some scientists tried to prevent Velikovsky's book from being published. His original publisher also had a large textbook business. Several scientists went to the publisher and threatened that if *Worlds in Collision* were not withdrawn, they would take their highly profitable textbooks elsewhere. The publisher caved in to the pressure. So Velikovsky merely took his manuscript down the street to another publisher who didn't have a textbook business. *Worlds in Collision* had already received an enormous amount of prepublication publicity, and when it was brought out by the second publisher it became an immediate, and huge, best seller.

Velikovsky could claim, with some justification, that an attempt had been made to suppress his book. Far from having the desired effect, this attempt at censorship made Velikovsky and his theories more famous and popular than ever. Velikovsky was seen as the champion of the independent thinker against the entrenched scientific establishment. Scientists are supposed to be champions of free inquiry. Why were they trying to keep Velikovsky from being heard? What did they have to hide? The public was confused.

The entire Velikovsky Affair had become a highly emotional issue within the scientific community. It made science look bad. Velikovsky's supporters—and he had a lot of active ones—pictured scientists as a group bent on destroying anyone who challenged any of their established theories. Scientists were shocked to discover just how many people were willing, even eager, to give credence to such a characterization.

Velikovsky continued to expand his theories in a series of popular books. Though he would never admit that he was wrong, even in the smallest detail, he did admit that some of his ideas were incomplete and kept promising that he would fill in the gaps in his later works. He never really did, but the original controversy over *Worlds in Collision* continued to provoke discussion for many years. Velikovsky and his supporters began to claim that science was coming over to his point of view, though the scientists denied it.

When *Worlds in Collision* first came out, Carl Sagan was still at Rahway High School. The controversy continued during his years at the University of Chicago and he often discussed Velikovsky with his colleagues. Sagan vividly recalls one conversation with a distinguished professor of Middle Eastern history, who said that all Velikovsky's historical scholarship was nonsense, but "I was impressed by the astronomy." Sagan commented, "I had rather the opposite view."

Finally, the American Association for the Advancement of Science (AAAS), at Sagan's urging, decided that it was time to bring the long-simmering Velikovsky controversy out into the open, and make it the subject of a full-scale symposium. After a great deal of patient negotiation, Velikovsky, who was by then a very old man and had always been an extremely difficult individual to deal with, finally agreed to participate. The symposium was held in February, 1974.

Sagan was delighted. "My own view is that no matter how unorthodox the reasoning process or how unpalatable the conclusions, there is no excuse for any attempt to suppress new ideas—least of all by scientists."

Sagan was to be a major participant in the discussion, not only because he already had a well-established reputation for explaining scientific ideas to the general public, but also because a couple of Velikovsky's most-cherished claims fell in areas where Sagan himself had a particular interest and expertize.

The debate between Sagan and Velikovsky was

a complex one, but it illuminates the difference between a scientific approach and one that simply sounds scientific.

A good deal of the debate turned on the high surface temperature of the planet Venus. It was a small point, certainly not central to Velikovsky's main arguments, but much had been made of it. Velikovsky said that the surface of Venus was "hot" because the planet had picked up heat when it passed close to the sun while it was a comet. Most astronomers of the 1940s predicted that the surface temperature of Venus would be fairly low. Later, when space probes discovered that the surface temperature was indeed high, Velikovsky loudly claimed that he had made a successful prediction, and his theory was the only one that could adequately explain the surface temperature of Venus.

Part of Sagan's doctoral thesis was concerned with the discovery of the higher than expected surface temperatures on Venus, so Sagan knew the subject and was able to analyze Velikovsky's claim carefully. He pointed out that Velikovsky had never specified how "hot" Venus was supposed to be. "Hot" is a very general word. Indeed, Velikovsky had never done any of the calculations that are routine for astronomers, apparently because he lacked the training to do so. Sagan, however, had performed the necessary calculations. He found that even if the planet Venus had passed close to the sun, as Velikovsky believed, it could never have received the sort of energy necessary to keep the surface "hot" to the present day. Any heat obtained from a passage close to the sun thousands of years ago would have long-since radiated away.

Velikovsky acknowledged that the planet's surface would be cooling slowly. There is no evidence that it is.

Even Velikovsky's claim that his prediction of a high temperature for Venus was original is highly suspect. In 1941, the astronomer Rupert Wildt had suggested in an article in the *Astrophysical Journal* that the surface temperature of Venus was much higher than conventional astronomers believed. Velikovsky, who "seems to have read all papers on Venus and Mars published in the *Astrophysical Journal* in the 1920s, 1930s, and 1940s, somehow overlooked this historically significant work." If he didn't overlook it, he certainly failed to mention it in *Worlds in Collision.*

Wildt proposed that a large abundance of carbon dioxide in the atmosphere of Venus was enough, through the greenhouse effect, to raise the surface temperature of the planet to around the normal boiling point of water. In the greenhouse effect on Venus, radiation from the sun is trapped by the atmospheric gases, thus raising the temperature on the surface. Most scientists now agree that it is the greenhouse effect that accounts for the high temperature of Venus, and Sagan is generally credited for updating Wildt's explanation, showing that the high radio brightness of Venus could be understood as a hot surface heated by a massive carbon dioxide/water greenhouse effect.

So Sagan showed that even on this point, which Velikovsky had trumpeted as one of his strongest, his theory and his method had failed.

Velikovsky was unpersuaded by the counterarguments of Carl Sagan and others. He died in 1979, still insisting that he was totally correct. But at least he could no longer claim that he had never been given a scientific hearing. His aging and dwindling band of followers continue to cling to generalized fragments of his theories; the specifics of the events during biblical times have largely been abandoned, even by the hard core of supporters.

Immanuel Velikovsky is no longer an emotional issue for the public or for scientists; his case has become an object lesson for scientists on how not to deal with the public.

For Sagan, "The UFO and Velikovsky issues are examples of a general concern I have about pseudoscience driving out science in the minds of the general public. It is the responsibility of scientists to respond to, not just ignore, pseudoscience."

CHAPTER FIVE

"This Is Not an Alien World"

When *Viking* sent back its first photographs from the surface of Mars, Carl Sagan sat transfixed before the monitor. "This is not an alien world," he thought. "I know places like it in Colorado and Arizona and Nevada." Sagan had not really expected to see a grizzled Martian prospector emerge from behind a Martian dune, leading a Martian mule; in fact, he would have been utterly shocked by such a sight. But somehow the image seemed appropriate to the scene that was being revealed by the Mars probe.

There was a moment while those early pictures were being transmitted that did provide a mild shock. What appeared to be the upper-case letter B seemed visible on one of the boulders. It turned out to be just a trick of the light, but, says Sagan, "There was just a moment when resounding in my head was the distant echo of a word from my boyhood—Barsoom."

New Yorker magazine writer Henry Cooper, who observed Sagan throughout the long preparations for the *Viking* project, noted that Sagan is a man "whose own childhood never seems very far behind him."

It was on Edgar Rice Burroughs' fictional Mars—Barsoom—where an eight-year-old Carl Sagan was first introduced to the possibility of life on other planets, particularly Mars.

The Burroughs' fantasies, the H. G. Wells famous invasion from Mars tale, *The War of the Worlds,* and a great deal of other life on Mars science fiction had been inspired by the work and the theories of the late nineteenth-century American astronomer, Percival Lowell. Lowell's career not only had a profound effect upon science fiction but on the scientific search for life on other worlds as well. Naturally, Sagan developed a great interest in this curious figure in the history of science.

Percival Lowell came from a wealthy and prominent Boston family. He was very much the gentleman scientist. He didn't have to make a living, but was able to pursue his interests, wherever they led. That's what the young Carl Sagan thought all astronomers had to be. What Lowell was chiefly interested in was the planet Mars, primarily because of all the planets in the solar system Mars seems the most Earthlike, and thus the most capable of supporting life.

Lowell was no idle dilettante or crankish eccentric. He was an astronomer of very real merit, who made genuine contributions to science. But what he is really remembered for is something that he was absolutely wrong about—the canals of the planet Mars.

In 1877 the Italian astronomer, Giovanni Schiaparelli, reported that he had observed a network of straight lines crisscrossing the surface of Mars. He called these lines *canali,* which in Italian means channels or grooves. "Channels" is a neutral term, but Schiaparelli's *canali* was translated into English as canals, a word that implies intelligent construction. All over the world astronomers and laymen alike were intrigued by "the canals of Mars," and no one was more fascinated than Percival Lowell.

Lowell was able to build his own observatory at Flagstaff, Arizona, where the atmosphere was relatively clear and unaffected by city lights. He spent much of the rest of his life peering through his 24-inch telescope at the surface of Mars. Over the years Lowell was able to map an intricate network of canals running from the poles across the entire surface of the planet.

At the turn of the century, astronomical observation was more of an art than a science. Even though Lowell had the best equipment available and an

Carl Sagan, 1979 *Photo by Bill Ray*

Sagan with *Viking* lander in Death Valley

Photo by Bill Ray

Plaque prepared for *Pioneer 10* space probe

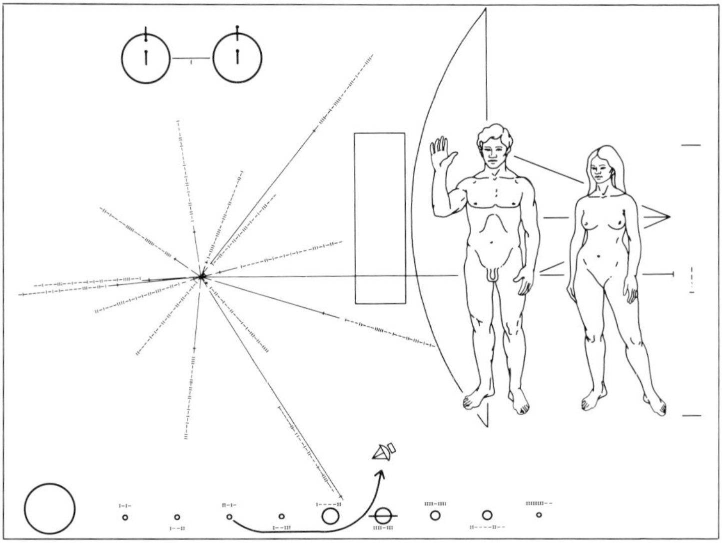

Sagan in front of the Great Sphinx with
replica of the Rosetta Stone *Photo by Bill Ray*

Sagan talks to students at his old public school
in Brooklyn, P.S. 101.

Sagan and
optical telescope

Photo by Bill Ray

Sagan and radio telescopes at Socorro, New Mexico
Photo by Bill Ray

Sagan relaxes at home with Ann Druyan.
© 1980 Tony Korody

Sagan and other protesters after their arrest at the Nevada Test Site *AP/Wide World Photos*

Carl Sagan *Brent Peterson*

excellent viewing location, the surface of Mars was not always clear. Most of the time the image was blurred and distorted. Then, for a few seconds, it would come into focus. The astronomer would have to remember what he saw during that brief period and sketch it on paper. There was a lot of room for interpretation and error. Other astronomers, professional and amateur, confirmed Lowell's observations of canals. But many more, using equipment as good as Lowell's, saw no canals at all. The canals of Mars were the subject of much dispute within the community of astronomers. The canals never showed up on photographs, but early astronomical photographs were never as good as the keen eye of the practiced observer.

While some astronomers may have disputed Lowell's canals, his prestige was great enough and his ideas so compelling that they took firm root in the mind and imagination of the general public. To Lowell, Mars was a planet covered by an Earth-like desert. The inhabitants of Mars, who were highly advanced technologically, had built a huge network of canals to bring water from the Martian poles to the rest of their parched planet. Lowell even thought he could detect seasonal changes in the color of vegetation along the canals.

In retrospect Lowell's canal theory seems pretty wild, and it contained some absolutely fatal flaws. If the planet was as dry as Lowell believed Mars to be, then any attempt to make the small supply of water travel vast distances in open canals would have been sheer madness. The water would evaporate away, or be soaked up by the parched ground. This problem for the canal theory was pointed out at the time, yet Lowell's ideas still gained a wide following. It was an era of spectacular canal building on Earth—the Suez canal in 1869, the Panama Canal in 1914. If we're doing it on Earth, people reasoned, why couldn't others have done it on Mars?

Lowell continued to cling to his canal theories until his death in 1916. However, fewer and fewer astronomers confirmed his observations, and by the time of his death, Lowell and his coworkers were practically the only remaining scientific supporters of the canal theory. But it continued to flourish in the popular imagination and the writings of fantasists like Edgar Rice Burroughs. Canals were a prominent feature of Barsoom. In that way Lowell profoundly influenced the life of Carl Sagan.

This is not to imply that the mature Carl Sagan ever believed in a network of artificially constructed canals on Mars. He was questioning Burroughs' science by the time he was nine. The canal theory itself had been crumbling as the result of repeated observations of the planet since 1916. Improved telescopes could find no hint of canals. The final demolition of Lowell's canals was provided by photographs taken by the *Mariner* space probes which skirted Mars and gave us the clearest and most remarkable pictures of the planet that had ever been seen. The *coup de grace* was provided by the *Mariner 9* probe in 1971, which photographed the whole planet, pole-to-pole with detail visible as small as one kilometer across. It was Sagan himself who wrote the paper that finally buried the canals of Mars forever. As with UFOs and Velikovsky, again Sagan confronted an exciting claim with skeptical scrutiny and scientific evidence and found it wanting. Still, the idea of life on the planet Mars had thoroughly captivated Sagan at an impressionable age, and he never quite lost his fascination.

Sagan tried to find out what Lowell saw, or thought he saw. After examining Lowell's original notebooks, Sagan felt that Lowell was a man "convinced that he had made an important discovery and distressed that others have not yet understood its significance." From Lowell's notebooks Sagan got the "distinct but uncomfortable feeling that he was really seeing something. But what?"

Lowell's maps, and the maps drawn by others who believed that they saw canals on the surface of Mars, were compared with photographs taken by *Mariner 9*. These photos were a thousand times better than anything Lowell might have seen with his earthbound telescope. "There is no doubt," says Sagan, "that what Lowell claimed to have seen is not on the planet." It has often been suggested that Lowell's eye strung together disconnected details in a straight line pattern. This Sagan doubts because there were no details to be strung together in the patterns Lowell said he observed.

Lowell was probably misled in part by his own desire to believe in life on Mars. But ultimately Sagan was puzzled by the canal problem. He feels that there is something essential that remains unknown, though the secret lies in the eye and mind of the observer and not on the surface of Mars.

While Lowell's passionate promotion of the canals of Mars and their intelligent origin made a great impression on the public at large, it ultimately alienated most of Lowell's scientific colleagues. Astronomers did not like to be closely associated with the tales of Edgar Rice Burroughs and H. G. Wells. The public's acceptance of the idea of intelligent life on Mars was so deep that when, in 1938, Orson Welles' radio version of the invasion from Mars story, *War of the Worlds,* was broadcast, it created a genuine panic. But by that time astronomers had virtually abandoned the hope of finding any life on nearby planets. When, as an undergraduate at the University of Chicago, Carl Sagan began seriously asking about the possibility of life on Mars there were very few scientists of reputation who would treat the subject seriously. One notable exception was Gerard Kuiper, Sagan's professor. Most older scientists had been turned off by Lowell's excesses. Some of the rising generation of scientists like Sagan had been turned on by the Lowell-inspired science fiction and fantasy.

The advent of space probes changed the general scientific attitude toward searching for life on Mars. During the 1960s NASA sent three probes, *Mariner 4, 6,* and *7,* past Mars. They photographed a small portion of the Martian surface. Then came *Mariner 9,* which photographed the entire planet. *Mariner 9* sent back pictures of unparalleled detail. Though they didn't show any canals or other signs of life, few scientists expected them to. A Martian photographic space probe passing the same distance from Earth would not necessarily have picked up any signs of life on this planet. The probes, however, gave scientists a chance to conduct a real search, and not merely speculate endlessly over possibilities.

The Soviets were also turning their attention to Mars. Between 1962 and 1973 the Soviets acknowledged that they had sent eight spacecraft toward the planet. U.S. space officials believe that they actually sent thirteen. The Soviet program, while ambitious, was not particularly successful. The Soviets were the first to actually land craft on the planet's surface, but these vehicles either were dead before they hit the surface or went dead immediately afterward without sending back any useful data. Some Soviet landers had arrived while Mars was in the midst of one of its enormous periodic planetwide dust storms. The storm may have contributed to the failure of the equipment, but even if those Soviet Mars landers had been working smoothly, they would not have been able to photograph much amid the planet's swirling dust.

The U.S. had its own plans to put an instrumented landing vehicle on Mars. Two probes, *Viking 1* and *2,* were to be launched in August and September of 1975. Each consisted of a lander, which was to descend to the surface of Mars, and an orbiter, which would continue to circle above it. The journey was to take eleven months and the first lander was scheduled to hit the surface of Mars on July 4, 1976—the day of the U.S. Bicentennial.

NASA hoped to avoid repeating the Soviet failures by constructing more flexible vehicles, ones that could respond to changing conditions like a major dust storm, and by careful planning. Indeed, the planning for the *Viking* missions began long before the Soviet failures occurred. When you are spending hundreds of millions of dollars to send a piece of highly sophisticated equipment into an unknown environment over 140 million miles away, you had better plan very, very carefully. Failure would not only be expensive, it would be well publicized. The civilian side of the U.S. space program has always depended on public support. A major failure would not only have hurt the Mars program but all scientific space research. Success, on the other hand, would generate a great deal of public interest and enthusiasm, and ultimately result in increased funding from the government.

As an astronomer with a special interest in the

planets, and particularly in Mars, Sagan was naturally asked to join one of the planning teams for the *Viking* project. But there was an even more compelling reason for having Sagan on the team; he was one of the very few astronomers with a solid background in biology, and one of the missions of the *Viking* lander was to look for signs of life on Mars. Sagan wasn't the only scientist interested in life on Mars. Among others on the *Viking* planning team was Sagan's friend and mentor, Joshua Lederberg.

Putting the *Viking* project together was an enormously complicated, and sometimes agonizing project. Sagan occasionally found himself the center of controversy. Many of those involved with *Viking*—astronomers, geologists, engineers, rocket scientists—either were not particularly interested in searching for life on Mars, or felt that the probability of finding anything was so low that the search was barely worth bothering about.

It wasn't that Sagan was convinced life would be found on Mars—far from it—but he certainly thought that it *might be,* that if it was there it would be very difficult to detect, and that it was very important to search for. Sagan passionately believed that every reasonable effort should be made to find life if it did exist, because that was one of the most exciting discoveries that modern science could possibly make. Sagan pointed out that the finding of life on Mars might revolutionize our knowledge of biology. Even *not* finding life, concluding that life definitely did not exist on Mars, would be important. "We then would have two similar nearby planets, one with life, one without. Why?"

Sagan, however, was extremely imaginative in his speculations about where life on Mars might be and how it could be detected. It wasn't just a natural stuffiness or an innate scientific conservatism that sometimes made Sagan's coworkers resist his ideas while planning *Viking*. They had solid, practical reasons. *Viking* was very expensive and a very crowded project. Every single extra ounce that was sent up cost huge sums of money. More significantly, there was a very strict limit on the number of experiments that could be crammed into the tiny *Viking* lander package. There were many more experiments proposed than there was space to hold them. If a biological project favored by Sagan was sent up, someone else's pet project would have to be bumped. Some other scientists also felt that even the time spent working up the instruments for a biological experiment they believed had only a remote chance of finding anything significant drew the efforts of scientists and engineers away from developing geological or other experiments they felt had a far greater chance of sending back important information. The arguments over what to put in the *Viking* lander were arguments over priorities. This sort of infighting is common to all space projects. For Sagan there was no higher priority, no more exciting task, than looking for life on other planets. But the whole process of deciding what was finally to go aboard *Viking* was, Sagan recalls, complex and difficult.

Detecting signs of life at a distance of 140 million miles figured to be an extremely difficult task. If the life was large enough—macrobes, the scientists call it—the task would, of course, be far simpler. If that grizzled old Martian prospector did walk out from behind a rock leading a Martian mule, *Viking*'s cameras would pick him up easily. But, while Carl Sagan expected life on Mars or elsewhere to have some basic similarities to life on Earth, he certainly didn't expect it to *look* like anything on Earth. "Never again in any place will there be people or cows or grass," he said. It is the variable and random nature of the evolutionary process that will prevent the development of familiar organisms in unfamiliar places. Even so, some unfamiliar forms would doubtless be quickly recognized as being alive.

"Suppose a fourteen-foot squamous purple ovoid with thirty tentacles came floating through the air, and *Viking* got a picture of it. We'd identify it as alive, even though we'd never seen it before and didn't know its chemistry."

There are, however, less improbable looking forms, that might be alive, or they might just be strangely shaped rocks, or some other natural but nonliving form. But what if the living creature moved very slowly, or conversely, what if a curious looking nonliving object was being blown about by the wind? Would the *Viking* cameras be able to detect a difference?

At one point Sagan rented a snake, a chameleon, and a couple of tortoises from a pet store and took them to Great Sand Dune National Monument in Colorado where a prototype of the *Viking* camera was being tested. The camera turned slowly and if the reptiles happened to be moving in the same direction, their images were greatly elongated. If they were moving in the opposite direction, they were compressed. The chameleon was too fast to be caught by the camera at all, but it did leave a nice set of footprints to be photographed. That got Sagan thinking.

The *Viking* camera was scheduled to be shut down during the cold Martian nights. Sagan was haunted by the thought that it would be turned on one morning and there would be a beautiful set of footprints, but no pictures of the creatures that made them! He wanted a light for the camera. This was an argument Sagan lost. The idea was vetoed. Remember, every inch of space and every ounce of weight aboard the *Viking* lander was precious. Other scientists figured that large forms of life on Mars were unlikely enough; that they would move around only during the frigid Martian night was even more unlikely.

If the *Viking* lander didn't detect any signs of

large life, that didn't necessarily mean that there wasn't any on Mars. It might only mean that the craft landed in a spot where there wasn't any large life. The landing sites had to be chosen primarily because they looked like safe places to land, not necessarily as the spots where life was most likely to exist. Said Sagan, "I came down in favor of spacecraft safety as the prime consideration even if it meant a lower probability of finding life." If the craft crashed, it wouldn't make any difference if it landed in an area teeming with Martian life; it couldn't send back any data.

Most of the scientists who worked on *Viking* believed that if life did indeed exist on Mars, it was most probably extremely small—microbes, not macrobes. The problems of detecting microscopic forms of life were far more daunting than those involved in detecting large forms of life. *Viking* couldn't photograph a microbe, and microbes don't leave footprints. Samples of the Martian surface could not be scooped up and sent back to Earth for analysis. *Viking* was making only a one-way trip.

One of Sagan's favorite Martian microbe tests had been developed by his friend and fellow life-on-Mars enthusiast, microbiologist Wolf Vishniac. The device was inevitably dubbed "The Wolf Trap." It would carry a small container of a nutrient solution to Mars. Then a sample of Martian soil would be mixed with it. The solution would be measured over a period of time to see if it grew cloudy. The assumption was that if it did, the Martian microbes were reproducing in the solution.

Vishniac began working on "The Wolf Trap" in the late 1950s and initially it was chosen as one of the four biological experiments to be aboard *Viking*. But in 1971 NASA cut back on the *Viking* biological experiments and "The Wolf Trap" was dropped. This was, in Sagan's words, a "crushing disappointment for Vishniac, who had invested twelve years in its development."

The three remaining microbiology experiments were designed to measure some aspect of the metabolism of Martian microbes, if there were any. As with "The Wolf Trap," samples of Martian soil would be scraped up by *Viking*'s remote arm, placed in a sealed container and then subjected to conditions that would presumably stimulate measurable biological activity. In one experiment the theoretical microbes would be presented with food to see if they ate it.

All three microbiology experiments were put in a black box that measured one foot on each side, weighed twenty pounds, and cost around 55 million dollars to develop and build.

The two American craft, *Viking 1* and *Viking 2,* were launched on schedule in August and September of 1975 on their eleven-month journey to the red planet. *Viking 1* missed its Bicentennial touchdown on Mars by sixteen days. As the craft was orbiting the planet's surface, it was determined that the original landing place was too risky, so the scientists decided to forego the symbolic value and look for a new and safer place to land. "A crash landing would have been an unsatisfactory two-hundredth birthday present for the United States," said Sagan.

The *Viking* landers proved to be absolute triumphs of careful planning and engineering. They worked better than anyone could reasonably have hoped. They sent back remarkable pictures of the surface of Mars that intrigued and excited the entire world. The *Viking* project was not merely a triumph of technology, it was a triumph of science as well. We now know more about Mars than we could have even dreamed of knowing a scant fifty years ago. But the *Viking* landers did not detect any signs of life, macrobe or microbe, on Mars.

There were some exciting moments at first when some of the experiments seemed to be sending back indications of biological activity. But closer examination of the results led to the conclusion that the suggestive results had probably been produced by inorganic processes. The generally negative results do not "prove" there is no life on Mars. But they have encouraged those who are skeptical of the possibility.

Indeed, the biological results from the *Viking* project were so discouraging that they have really put a chill on hopes of finding life on any nearby planets. Though the *Viking* landers were technically and scientifically a huge success, there have been no immediate follow-ups in the U.S. space program. Overall, the civilian space program has been severely cut back since the heady days of the early 1970s. Sagan feels this is primarily because of the "preoccupation of the United States with manned and military activities rather than with scientific exploration." But if there had been any reasonable hope that further probes really would detect life on Mars, it is almost certain that they would have been launched, no matter what the cost.

The possible failure of *Viking* to detect any signs of life on Mars has even influenced the thinking of some scientists about the possibility of finding life anywhere else in the Universe. Some have come to the conclusion that if not even the lowest form of life exists on the planet in our solar system that, aside from Earth, had generally been assumed to be most likely to contain it, then perhaps life does not develop so easily and the conditions on our planet are truly unique. There had always been a group of scientists who believed that we may be quite alone in our galaxy, or that life elsewhere may be so rare and distant as to be virtually undetectable. Before *Viking,* all the talk was of life proliferating throughout the galaxy. Now the doubters have gained some converts and their voices are heard more often.

Sagan insists he is not emotionally wedded to the idea of abundant life in the galaxy. The problem of extraterrestrial life is a deeply important one to him. "But in science we must courageously follow the evidence where it takes us, and not foist our own predispositions on the Universe." A number of his planetary studies have led him to conclusions which make life on nearby planets seem less rather than more likely. The aim, he says, is not to "prove" that there is extraterrestrial life, but to search for it, as dilligently and carefully as possible.

But he has certainly not joined the ranks of those who seriously doubt the existence of extraterrestrial life anywhere. Sagan remains the optimist and the enthusiast. He has even found flickers of hope that life may yet be detected on Mars. His friend and fellow enthusiast, Wolf Vishniac, went to the most Marslike environment on Earth, the dry valleys of the Antarctic. Previous investigators had determined that there were no native microbes in this extremely hostile environment. Using new types of equipment, however, Vishniac was able to discover a wide variety of microbes, including some that actually lived inside the rocks.

Tragically, Wolf Vishniac was killed during an Antarctic expedition in 1973.

Just because microbes can surprise us and live inside of Antarctic rocks does not mean that they do or even could live inside of Martian rocks. The dry valleys of the Antarctic are "Marslike" but they are certainly not Mars. There has been a resurgence of interest in life on Mars recently, mainly because there now seems to be good evidence that a billion years ago there was abundant flowing water on Mars.

Sagan still insists that the *Viking* biological experiments represent only a "pioneering first effort; they hardly represent a definitive search for life on Mars." However, he concludes that at present there is "no compelling evidence for microbiology on Mars."

But Martian microbes or not, Carl Sagan still has an irresistible interest in Mars. There has been a pause in the attempts to explore Mars, but he points out that major Martian exploration is by no means dead. The U.S. space program has been disrupted by a series of accidents during 1986. However, there are still plans to launch a Mars *Observer* satellite by the end of the decade. The Soviets appear to be planning an ambitious program of Martian exploration over the next few years. Sagan believes that if the two superpowers pool their knowledge and resources and cooperate, we may be able to send a manned expedition to Mars early in the next century.

Then if one of those "squamous purple ovoids with thirty tentacles" happens to be floating around, we will be able to get a look at it firsthand.

CHAPTER SIX

The Brain

On a visit to the *Musee de l'Homme,* the Museum of Man, in Paris, Carl Sagan and Ann Druyan found themselves in a roomful of brains. That does not mean that they were in a roomful of smart people, it means that they were in a roomful of real brains—human brains floating in bottles.

In the often dank and musty back sections of the museum, where research was carried out and where objects not on display were stored, Sagan wandered through rooms full of bones and skulls. He cautiously handled a reconstructed Neanderthal skull, "perhaps the first compelling piece of evidence that there once were creatures rather like us who became extinct . . ."

Beyond the bones were "more macabre and more

disturbing collections." There were a couple of shrunken heads, jars of human embryos and fetuses, and a collection of large bottles containing human heads. "Men and women and children of both sexes and many races, decapitated, their heads shipped to France" for study.

Then in an even more obscure spot he found shelf upon shelf of human brains, stored in formalin-filled bottles to preserve them. The bottles contained the brains of everyone from intellectuals to murderers; a cross section of humanity. In the late nineteenth century, when this particular collection was begun, many scientists believed that by observing and measuring the human brain they would be able to learn something significant about human behavior. It was hoped, for example, that there would be an identifiable type of "criminal brain." Then it could be assumed that murder or other crimes were a matter of simple heredity, a comforting thought for those reluctant to consider that failures in social institutions might be responsible for crime. This hope went unrealized, for except in cases of gross brain malformation, the brain of the murderer and the brain of the saint were indistinguishable in the days in which the collection was established, and in our own as well. There may be physiological differences, but we don't know what they are. "It is, very probably, society and not heredity that makes criminals," Sagan commented.

Among the many bottled brains gathering dust

on the shelves of that French museum was one labeled P. Broca. It was the brain of Paul Broca, the late nineteenth-century French scientist who had actually begun this collection of brains and heads and much else that was stored in the *Musee de l'Homme.* The experience of finding Broca's brain set off a chain of reflections and speculations in Carl Sagan's and Ann Druyan's minds. These resulted ultimately in one of his most striking essays titled, appropriately enough, *Broca's Brain.* It also became the title piece in a 1979 book of essays on science.

Sagan's first reaction to this macabre collection was a distinctly negative one. It seemed callous, a rather brutal attempt to establish the biological inferiority of certain races, nations, and classes. Such attempts were common in Broca's day, and unfortunately still exist in our day as well. Broca, whose history Sagan knew, certainly reflected many of the beliefs and values of his time, but he was not "more of a jingoist and a racist than most." He was also not the sort of Dr. Frankenstein-like scientist, who coldly pursues his work regardless of the human consequences. "Broca," says Sagan, "very much cared."

Broca was passionately committed to free scientific inquiry, so much so that he was often in trouble with government and religious authorities. Yet he was still unable to cast off many of the prejudices of his age. Sagan realized that Broca could not be criticized for being of his own time, but in contemplating the nineteenth-century scientist's career he found that it raised "nagging uncertainties about which of the conventional truths of our own age will be considered unforgivable bigotry by the next." The only solution that Sagan saw to this dilemma "is to challenge, deeply and seriously, our own most strongly held beliefs." That is not the sort of suggestion that makes people very comfortable.

Scientific inquiry carries risks, because there is no guarantee that things are going to turn out the way we want them to. But it is a risk we must take, said Sagan, because there is no other way of dealing with the Universe.

Of course, there can be abuses in the pursuit of scientific knowledge. The best way to avoid them, insists Sagan, returning to another of his familiar themes, "is for the population to be scientifically literate, to understand the implications of such investigations. In exchange for freedom of inquiry, scientists are obliged to explain their work. If science is considered a closed priesthood, too difficult and arcane for the average person to understand, the dangers of abuse are greater."

Sagan was not prowling around back rooms of the *Musee de L'Homme* as a mere tourist; he did not wander amidst the severed heads and bottled brains out of morbid curiosity alone. Indeed, he found somewhat to his surprise that the collection made him feel distinctly uncomfortable. He wondered if such fears were not born deep in our evolutionary past when the presence of severed heads or other isolated body parts might be an indication of danger. Those who avoided places where such objects were collected might be more likely to survive and thus leave more offspring. "Experiencing such fears bestows an evolutionary advantage."

Sagan had come to the museum because he has a long-standing interest in the history and development of science, and because he has a particular interest in the development of the human brain. Sagan's first major popular success in writing was a book called *The Dragons of Eden: Speculation on the Evolution of Human Intelligence. Dragons,* published in 1977, spent thirty-three weeks on the *New York Times* best-seller list, and grabbed a flock of writing prizes for Sagan, including the very prestigious Pulitzer Prize for general nonfiction.

Sagan was no expert in this area of science. He had training in biology, and had a long-standing interest in the origin of life, but he admitted that he had little formal training in subjects like the anatomy and physiology of the brain—and these subjects are difficult. Yet Sagan couldn't resist the intellectual challenge, to find out about, and to write about, areas of science that were new to him. The challenge came when he was asked to deliver the first Jacob Bronowski Memorial Lecture in Natural Philosophy in November, 1975. The lecture was established in honor of the recently deceased British scientist/philosopher/poet, Jacob Bronowski. Shortly before his death Bronowski had hosted a very popular science television series called "The Ascent of Man." Sagan called it a "superb teaching tool and a remarkable memorial." This series was to profoundly influence Sagan's own "Cosmos" series a few years later.

The subject of the lecture was to be the evolution of intelligence. It was not just an esoteric topic to Sagan. "A better understanding of the nature and evolution of human intelligence just possibly might help us to deal intelligently with our unknown and perilous future." And, of course, it was connected with the question of extraterrestrial intelligence.

Sagan admitted to approaching the subject with "a considerable degree of trepidation," because he was no expert. He also said that many of his ideas were "speculative." But Carl Sagan is nothing if not intellectually bold. The lecture was well received, and Sagan was encouraged to expand his ideas into the book that was to win him a Pulitzer prize.

Sagan started with some basic principles. He is an evolutionist. Evolution by natural selection he calls "the great organizing principle of modern biology." The human brain has evolved like any other organ system. Those individuals that possessed slightly superior brains gained an evolutionary advantage over their less well favored contemporaries, and by natural selection the size and the capabilities of the human brain grew rapidly.

Another fundamental premise is that the brain is a physical organ: "The workings—what we sometimes call 'mind'—are a consequence of its [the brain's] anatomy and physiology, and nothing more."

Much of *The Dragons of Eden* is a clear and fairly straightforward popular account of the best scientific information and theory concerning the structure and development of the brain available at that time. For the uninstructed, the book provided a good basic introduction to brain biology. But the real delights of *The Dragons of Eden* are the speculations, the intellectual sparks that fly from Sagan's own brain when he comes in contact with an intriguing concept or theory.

Take the title of the book, for example. Sagan sees in the biblical story of the Garden of Eden an "appropriate metaphor" for some of the events in humanity's biological history. Is this accidental? Sagan very gently suggests at least the possibility that some sort of biological memory may be stored in our genetic code. That means we might have some sort of "memory" of things experienced by our distant ancestors even before they were fully human.

"Perhaps the Garden of Eden is not so different from Earth as it appeared to our ancestors of some three or four million years ago, during a legendary golden age when the genus *Homo* was perfectly interwoven with the other beasts and vegetables."

In the Bible the Fall was the result of eating the fruit of the tree of knowledge. It was not the acquisition of general knowledge that was forbidden, "but, specifically, the knowledge of the difference between good and evil—that is, abstract and moral judgments," says Sagan. Such judgments can only be made with the development of that portion of the brain called the neocortex—the last portion of the human brain to evolve and that part of the brain that gives us the mental qualities that define us as distinctly human.

One of the punishments for eating fruit from the tree of knowledge was "In pain shalt thou [Eve] bring forth children." Sagan said that childbirth is not painful for many species, but may be for humans because of the enormous and rapid increase in the size of the human skull. A larger skull is needed to contain a larger brain.

Another punishment for knowledge was death. While death was certainly not a result of brain evolution, awareness of death probably was. "One of the earliest consequences of the anticipatory skills that accompanied the evolution of the prefrontal lobes must have been the awareness of death. Man is probably the only organism on Earth with a relatively clear view of the inevitability of his own end."

That takes care of the Eden in the book title, but what about the dragons? Here again Sagan plunged into what he freely admitted was highly speculative theory. Speculative it may be, but it is also very stimulating. He pointed out that myths of reptilelike dragons are pervasive in both East and West. There is St. George and the dragon and the Chinese dragon. Sagan wondered whether large reptiles might have threatened our protohuman ancestors a few million years ago, and that the terror somehow carried over into the myths of the dragon. Or perhaps the dragons of myth are somehow related to the ancient "reptilian" parts of our brain. "When we feared the dragons, were we fearing a part of ourselves?"

A frequently speculated-upon source for the dragon myth are the reptilelike dinosaurs. Sagan pointed out that dinosaurs became extinct some sixty-five million years ago, well before any protohumans existed. Yet even here he wondered if some of the dinosaurs might have escaped extinction for millions of years. Perhaps a few were encountered at some point by manlike creatures and left a lasting impression. Could some of these dinosaurs somehow have contributed to our pervasive dreams and fears of "monsters," he asked.

The dinosaurs were probably extinct far too early to contribute anything to human myths and fears, but dinosaurs do figure prominently in Sagan's speculations. He noted that if the dinosaurs had not died out, apparently suddenly and mysteriously at the end of the period called the Cretaceous, then the mammals, including our distant ancestors, would probably never have come to dominate the Earth.

But why did the dinosaurs die? Today there has been much talk of the catastrophic destruction of dinosaurs due to massive climate changes resulting from the impact of a large meteorite or comet with the Earth. In the 1980s Sagan has come to look at this possibility in a very different context. But back in 1975 while the extinction of the dinosaurs was regarded as a mystery by most scientists, it was not widely discussed. Often the extinction was attributed vaguely to "climate changes." Sagan, however, was intrigued by the hypothesis advanced by his Soviet colleague I. S. Shklovskii (Sagan's coauthor of *Intelligent Life in the Universe*). Shklovskii suggested that a gigantic stellar explosion, a supernova, bombarded the Earth with an immense flux of high energy charged particles, and it was this bombardment that led to the death of the dinosaurs. The meteorite hypothesis has more evidence to support it today, but to seriously discuss any theory involving an extraterrestrial catastrophe in 1975 was bold indeed.

If the dinosaurs had not died off, Sagan wondered whether the dominant forms of life on Earth today would be descendants of the more intelligent dinosaurs. Would they be "writing and reading books, speculating on what would have happened if the mammals prevailed?"

All sorts of things about the brain captured Sagan's restless attention. Why do we sleep? In fact, no one really knows. Early mammals may have slept during the day, when the dinosaurs were active. Staying very quiet and out of sight would have been necessary for the survival of tiny mammals in the era of dinosaurs. Later, when the mammals prevailed, some—like our own ancestors—changed from daytime to nighttime sleepers. Even today, some mammals are active at night and sleep during the day. Sagan wondered if one day people will not evolve to the point where they need little if any sleep. "I for one freely confess envy for such an adaptation," he wrote.

Dreams fascinated him. Why do we dream? What, if anything, do our dreams mean? Sagan related one of his own dreams, one he said will "tantalize me forever." He is reading a thick history book. The chapters are arranged chronologically. He reads about Greece and Rome, the Middle Ages, the Renaissance, coming closer and closer to modern times. When he gets through World War II he realizes that there are still hundreds of pages left to read. "With mounting excitement I worked my way more deeply into the work until I was sure I had passed my own time." But when it came to reading the future he couldn't do it. He could make out the letters, but he couldn't put the letters together in words or sentences. Somehow that seems like the sort of a dream Carl Sagan would have.

Sagan said he often dreams of being unable to read, and in his dreams he can't perform even simple mathematical tasks either.

How far back do individual memories go? Sagan said, "At age three, my son Nicholas was asked for the earliest event he could recall and replied in a hushed tone while staring into middle distance, 'It was red, and I was very cold.' He was born by Caesarian section." Sagan was unsure whether this was a true "birth memory," but it made him wonder.

Sagan was impressed by the apparent intelligence of many of the nonhuman primates like chimpanzees, and by the brains of whales and dolphins. What should our moral posture be in regard to these intelligent animals? Sagan said it should probably include "firm strictures against at least the gratuitous slaughter of these animals."

But if apes are so smart—and Sagan spent a good deal of space in *The Dragons of Eden* discussing the intelligence of apes—why can't they talk? Why don't they, or any other living creatures aside from humans, have a real language? Complex language seems to be a uniquely human attribute. But experiments that Sagan described in detail have shown that apes, like chimpanzees, are just on the edge of language. But why just on the edge? Why didn't some other species pass over the edge? "One possible answer, it seems to me, is that humans have systematically exterminated those other primates who displayed signs of intelligence." That is a rather disturbing thought.

Intelligence, Sagan said, is the "essential human quality." By intelligence he doesn't mean being what is popularly called "smart" as opposed to what is called "dumb." Intelligence is the "development and functioning of the neocortex," that most uniquely human part of the brain.

This led Sagan to a discussion of the highly emotional subject of abortion. It can't really be about a "right to life," he argued, because we destroy living things all the time. The point must be a right to *human* life. Perhaps an "acceptable compromise in the abortion debate," he said, could be arrived at by determining when the brain develops a distinctly human character. On the basis of embryological and brain wave evidence, he suggested, "perhaps the transition would fall toward the end of the first trimester or near the beginning of the second trimester of pregnancy."

Sagan was fascinated by the effectiveness of some tranquilizers and other antipsychotic drugs in treating certain forms of mental illness. That led him to discussing a study conducted in the 1960s at the Harvard Medical School. A group of psychiatrists performed a set of experiments on the relative value of their therapies and drugs in treating the mental disorder schizophrenia. Before the experiment the psychiatrists had believed that the best way of curing the problem was by talking about the patient's early childhood experiences. It turned out that the drugs were much more effective, and the psychiatrists honestly reported this fact. Sagan found the integrity of the experimenters in the face of this completely unexpected result "breathtaking." "It is difficult to imagine any experiment that would convince leading practitioners of many political or religious philosophies of the superiority of a competing doctrine."

Our species attains maturity very slowly, compared to all other animal species. This gives us a long time in which to learn. Sagan reflected on the life of Jacob Bronowski, and a number of other scientist/scholars whose accomplishments ranged widely over a variety of areas. Sagan approvingly quoted one of these scientist/scholars, Bertrand Russell, who said that the development of such gifted individuals required a long period during childhood in which there was little or no pressure for conformity. The child is allowed to develop his or her own interests. Sagan suggested that the current pressures for conformity are making such individuals increasingly rare.

In an essay in the book *Broca's Brain,* Sagan talked about the childhood and education of one of his favorite people, Albert Einstein. Einstein, he noted, was a poor student, primarily because he rebelled against the rigid and mechanized methods of teaching in Germany in the 1890s. Sagan admired Einstein's genius, and his nonconformity. "Had he [Einstein] been a teenager in the 1960s and 1970s rather than the 1890s, conventional people would almost certainly have called him a hippie," wrote Sagan.

Einstein's opinions of the educational methods of his own time were scathing. He found rote learning the enemy of curiosity. Sagan wondered whether some of the same criticisms might be applicable to education today. "How many potential Einsteins have been permanently discouraged through competitive examinations and the forced feeding of curricula?"

Sagan also noted with great approval that Einstein spoke of "an excellent popular exposition" of science that he read while a teenager, that helped him tremendously in his self-education. Popularizers of science take heart, said Sagan.

At the end of *The Dragons of Eden,* Carl Sagan turned once again to one of his most compelling interests, the search for extraterrestrial intelligence. It is a subject that he had already discussed exhaustively in other works. But as usual he had something new and stimulating to say. One of the benefits of receiving a message from an advanced extraterrestrial civilization would be to prove that there are advanced civilizations that can live with advanced technology without destroying themselves. "Finding a solution to a problem is helped enormously by the certain knowledge that a solution exists. This is one of the many curious connections between the existence of intelligent life elsewhere and the existence of intelligent life on Earth."

The future of our species, Sagan asserted, depends on how well we use our highly evolved brain. "We are unlikely to survive if we do not make full and creative use of our human intelligence."

CHAPTER SEVEN

"Cosmos"

The project started in a modest enough way. Carl Sagan was dismayed that space probes like *Mariner* and *Viking* received so little attention on television. Here were subjects that were not only scientifically important and interesting, but they were visually exciting as well. They should have been perfect fare for television, Sagan believed; instead, they were virtually ignored. Sagan was well aware of the power of television, which he calls "one of the grandest teaching tools ever invented, particularly for teaching science."

So Sagan began looking around for a sponsor for a series of programs on space exploration. What he finally got was an agreement with KCET, the Los Angeles Public Television station, for a 13-part series that covered the scientific exploration of just about everything from the world of the atom to the edge of the Universe. Along the way it also touched on philosophy, religion, politics, art, and history. The all-encompassing title for this all-encompassing series was to be "Cosmos." The series may have been the single most successful attempt at the popularization of science in history.

Sagan insists that "Cosmos" was anything but a one-man production. The "Cosmos" staff was about 150 people. His cowriters, Ann Druyan and Steven Soter, can be singled out for their impressive contributions to the success of the series. But Carl Sagan was the one in front of the cameras. He was the name and he was the face, as far as the public was concerned. "Cosmos" was the project that really made Carl Sagan an international celebrity.

There had been models for the "Cosmos" series. One was British art historian Lord Kenneth Clark's "Civilisation," produced by the British Broadcasting Corporation. (The British always spell the word with an "s" and when the series was shown in the United States the "s" was retained, perhaps for snob value.) It was an attempt to trace the history of civilization, primarily through art and architecture. The very aristocratic Lord Clark had a rather casual attitude toward the series. He thought of it as rather a lightweight trifle, and was as surprised as anyone when it became a major popular success not only in Britain but on Public Broadcasting stations throughout the U.S. as well. A series which centered on an English lord wandering around museums and monasteries declaiming on art styles in his very upper-class accent seemed unlikely popular TV fare. Yet somehow it caught on.

Emboldened by this unlikely success, the BBC launched an even more ambitious project, "The Ascent of Man." The creator and narrator of this series was the German-born scientist/philosopher/poet, Jacob Bronowski. For people who had slept through science education films in school and found the "Mr. Wizard" type of science TV show boring, Bronowski was a revelation. The production was often visually stunning. Instead of a string of filmed experiments, Bronowski took his viewers to the patent office in Berne, Switzerland, where the young Albert Einstein had worked when he conceived his most brilliant ideas. The Theory of Relativity was illustrated in the streets of the city where the theory was born. Bronowski discussed the mathematical concepts of Pythagoras and Euclid on the shores of the Greek isles. You didn't have to film a discussion of the mathematics of the Greeks in Greece, but it made good television.

Bronowski was extremely intelligent, energetic, emotional, and wide-ranging in his interests. Even people who did not completely understand what was going on were swept up in the host's obvious enthusiasm and the pace and sheer beauty of the series. "Ascent of Man" was a huge success, not only in Britain and America, but throughout the world. It was science popularization as it had never been done before.

This was the sort of show that KCET and Sagan wished to pattern the "Cosmos" series after. "Ascent"'s British producer, Adrian Malone, was hired to oversee the project. But "Cosmos" was not to be a mere carbon copy of "Ascent" on a cosmic scale, it was to be an entirely original production. While Sagan attributes much of the success of the series to his cowriters, who were equal partners in the venture, he was the on-screen star.

The success of "Civilisation" and "The Ascent of Man" rested heavily on the screen images of Lord Clark and Jacob Bronowski. Clark was detached and slightly ironic, Bronowski restless and passionate. Both were enormously appealing, and they would be tough acts to follow. Comparisons would certainly be made.

Sagan presented a very different image. He was casual and professorial, dressed primarily in a corduroy jacket and turtleneck jersey. But he was also good looking, possessing what writer Robert F. Moss calls "dark-eyed sensual handsomeness . . . sex appeal."

Sagan, of course, had television experience, but to be successful in a dozen guest shots on the "Tonight" show is one thing, to succeed as the host of a series like "Cosmos" was something else again. Sagan would be on screen almost constantly. Shooting was to be done all over the world, in brief segments. Yet the overall effect had to be flowing and seamless. Though he had to stick to a carefully prepared script, and had to go over scenes again and again, he always had to look and sound natural and fresh. Any hint of woodenness and artificiality, and the illusion of a very comfortable Sagan talking directly and informally to each individual viewer would be destroyed, and the project, no matter how well produced it might otherwise be, would fail. It was a task experienced actors would find daunting.

The project absorbed much of Sagan's energy for three years. In 1979 he took time away from "Cosmos" to participate in the *Voyager 1* and *2* encounters with Jupiter. Things were also happening in his personal life that made the work more difficult. Sagan's parents had moved to California to live with him during the production of "Cosmos." Early in the filming Sagan discovered that his father, Samuel, had developed lung cancer. The disease progressed rapidly and in less than a year Samuel Sagan was dead. Carl often had to spend days away from filming to be with his parents, and the emotional strain was great.

Sagan's second marriage had dissolved. He and Linda had been legally separated since 1977; the divorce was finalized in 1981. By that time Sagan was a real celebrity, and his divorce was given the sort of publicity usually reserved for movie stars. The property settlement was widely reported as $1 million or more, but Sagan insists this figure is wildly exaggerated, and there was nowhere near that kind of money involved.

Since the separation Sagan and Ann Druyan had been inseparable. The two had first met in 1974 and worked together closely on "Cosmos." "She wrote it with me and Steve Soter," says Sagan. Carl and Ann were married in 1981, just a month after his divorce became final. The book *Cosmos* is dedicated to Ann Druyan. "In the vastness of space and the immensity of time, it is my joy to share a planet and an epoch with Annie."

So the work on "Cosmos" did not come at the easiest or most tranquil time in Carl Sagan's life. The project itself was far from a simple one. There were the disagreements and disputes that inevitably arise during a complex and lengthy endeavor like "Cosmos." Sagan had been in front of the cameras before but as far as TV production was concerned he was a novice. However, he was not content to remain one for long. He was constantly asking questions and making suggestions to the production crew.

And, of course, there were enormous logistical problems. Filming had to be carried out all over the world. In order to simulate the landing of the *Viking* space probes on the surface of Mars, the "Cosmos" crew used the barren, Marslike surface of Death Valley where the original *Viking* lander had been tested. However, there was a snowstorm which disrupted the schedule. The Air Force was conducting bombing runs at a nearby test range, and every time a flight went over, filming had to stop. In fact, the precarious political and military situation on this planet consistently intruded itself into this very cosmic project.

In order to film on the sites where some of the great scientific discoveries were made, the "Cosmos" crew visited Alexandria, Egypt, and the Aegean island of Samos. In Alexandria the hotel in which they stayed was the object of practice strafing runs by the Egyptian Air Force. In Greece permission to film anywhere was delayed until the last moment because of NATO maneuvers. In some countries the crew was shadowed by suspicious security agents. Permission to do any filming in Kaluga, USSR, home of the Russian astronautics pioneer Konstantin Tsiolkovsky, was denied because a trial of dissidents was being conducted there. Sagan was struck by the enormity of the world's military presence, and by the fact that there was so much fear in the hearts of nations. In his introduction to the book "Cosmos," Sagan wrote, "The experience confirms my resolve to treat, when relevant, social questions both in the series and in the book."

Despite the "earthly" problems in filming "Cosmos," there were even greater difficulties imposed by the very nature of the series. "Cosmos" had to make visual and engrossing things that we can really only imagine. Lord Clark had been able to use Florence and London as backdrops for "Civilisation." For "The Ascent of Man," Jacob Bronowski could stand on the plains of Africa or at the site of a Nazi concentration camp. Sagan could be at the Cavendish Laboratories in Cambridge, England, in Chola temples in South India, on the island of Samos, and some forty other earthly locations, but a major part of the series was set out there among the stars. Creating the feeling of being in space without making the series appear either to be a dull "educational" film or pure science fiction was the greatest challenge faced by Sagan, his cowriters, and the entire "Cosmos" crew.

Ultimately there were scenes with a distinct science fiction appearance to them. There was Carl Sagan piloting a spaceship that looked, to *Time* magazine anyway, like "something by H. G. Wells out of Walt Disney."

The series made lavish use of photographs taken either by earthbound observatories or space probes. Many of these images, like those of Jupiter taken by the *Voyager* spacecraft, were familiar but to many viewers, including this writer, they still retained an awe-inspiring quality, particularly because you knew they were real.

Other production techniques were used. When he discussed the landing of *Viking* on Mars, Sagan stood in the Marslike environment of California's Death Valley in front of a model of the *Viking* craft. The similarity between Death Valley and what was seen in the pictures of the Martian surface returned by *Viking* was striking. Sagan recalled his thoughts on first viewing the *Viking* pictures of the Martian surface, "This is not an alien world."

But there are truly alien worlds that had to be shown as well; many of these could only be artists' conceptions. Sagan and his staff worked meticulously with the artists to make sure galaxies, stars, and planets were portrayed not just attractively, but accurately.

One of the most striking segments of "Cosmos" showed a Jupiter-like planet where the dense atmosphere was populated with alien life forms called "floaters" and "hunters." The "floaters" and the "hunters" were conceived as the result of a set of detailed calculations that Sagan made along with Cornell colleague, E. E. Salpeter. The calculations on which these theoretical life forms were based had been published in proper scientific form in the *Astrophysical Journal.* The "floaters" and "hunters" were not the product of imagination alone.

In addition to the construction of other worlds, there were some historical reconstructions as well. The most spectacular was Ann Druyan's concept of the great library at Alexandria in Egypt, one of the great repositories of ancient knowledge. There was Carl Sagan rummaging through long-lost papyrus scrolls. Since we really have no detailed knowledge of what the famous library actually looked like—it was completely destroyed during Roman times and surviving descriptions are sketchy at best—this scene was based on educated speculation.

There were criticisms that centered primarily around the dominant, indeed overwhelming, role that Sagan played in the series. He was always center stage. The camera lingered on his handsome face a great deal of the time. This led to some complaints that he was arrogant and egotistical. Though Sagan exercised a great deal of control over "Cosmos," his control was not total and he has always said that all of the "interminable close-ups of me looking awed" were not his idea, and that they were "presented by the producers as a *fait accompli.*"

Popular legend has it that Carl Sagan repeated the phrase "billions and billions" several times during the episodes. "Billions and billions of stars," "billions and billions of years," and so on. It became a joke. Johnny Carson would put on his Carl Sagan wig and intone "billions and billions," and the "Tonight" audience would break up. But Sagan never actually used the phrase "billions and billions" in "Cosmos," people just think he did. It doesn't matter anymore; the words will be forever identified with him. A cartoon by Gary Larson, creator of *The Far Side,* has "Carl Sagan as a kid" pointing to the sky and saying, "Just look at all those stars, Becky. There must be *hundreds* of 'em."

Not all of the episodes of "Cosmos" showed Sagan in exotic or fantastical settings. For one he returned to his old Brooklyn school, P.S. 101, to deliver a lecture on astronomy to a new generation of students. The sequence showed that even in the simple setting of an ordinary public school classroom Sagan can be an impressively charismatic teacher.

It took nearly three years to film the thirteen episodes of "Cosmos" and the filming involved a production staff of 150 people and was shot at forty different locations in twelve countries. The total cost for production and promotion was $8.5 million. In the world of big-time film making that is not such a huge figure. Even a mediocre sci-fi epic will have a production budget in excess of $10 million. But "Cosmos" was a Public Television series, an educational series, and as such the $8.5 million budget was unprecedented.

"Cosmos" was a huge gamble for Public Television and for Carl Sagan personally. He had, after all, invested the better part of three years in it. If it flopped it would have been a noble, but expensive, failure. But the gamble paid off more handsomely than anyone had imagined or even hoped. If the show didn't attract "billions and billions" of viewers, it certainly attracted "millions and millions." In fact, it attracted more viewers than any other regular series in the history of the Public Broadcasting System.

The shows were educational but they were also enormously entertaining and involving. They attracted and held not only the scientifically inclined, but a large number of those who couldn't care less about science. I well remember my own eleven-year-old daughter, whose interest in science was minimal, dropping everything on Sunday night so that she could watch Carl Sagan on TV. Like most viewers of "Cosmos," I doubt if she understood everything that was being presented. But she was led by Sagan's enthusiasm into the wonder of science. Suddenly science was more than just a collection of facts to be learned for a test (and then quickly forgotten). It was exciting. It was fun. Carl Sagan was as much fun for her as Edgar Rice Burroughs must have been for a young Carl Sagan.

My own reaction was awe, mixed, I must admit, with a touch of envy. As a sometime writer of popular science, I have always believed that the key to involving the nonscientist was to excite his or her imagination. That's what I had tried to do, and here was Carl Sagan doing it so much better than I had ever dreamed of. It wasn't just that he was a celebrity scientist with a high-priced TV production staff to back him up, it was the quality of his own passion for the subject that made all the difference. He also respected the intelligence of his nonscientist audience. The series was flat-out good.

"There is nothing about science that cannot be explained to the layman," Sagan insists. He might have added, "if you know how."

"Cosmos" goes on and on. It is still being shown worldwide and has been seen now in more than sixty nations by more than 300 million people. An updated version is currently making the rounds of U.S. channels in syndication. That is the sort of record that Lucille Ball could be proud of. The series picked up three Emmys and a Peabody and a flock of other awards and commendations. But the greatest award was that people liked it, they watched it, and they learned from it. The accompanying book, also called *Cosmos,* is the best-selling science book in the history of the English language.

Before "Cosmos," Carl Sagan had been a celebrity scientist; after "Cosmos" he has become a scientist superstar. He is now instantly recognized wherever he goes throughout the world. He is the object of autograph hunters and curiosity seekers, but unlike many other stars, he does not complain about the price of fame.

How about the parodies, the Carl Sagan wigs, the intoning of "billions and billions"? "Look, anyone who is really upset by that kind of thing has the option of not being a public figure," he says.

One aspect of fame that has bothered Sagan a bit is that he feels the success of "Cosmos" and other popularizations have sometimes tended to obscure the work he has done as a scientist and teacher. That is probably inevitable, but it still makes Sagan uncomfortable.

Though rumors of grumbling among scientists about the Sagan ego and of his tendency to blur the line between speculation and fact have occasionally appeared in the press, Sagan says that none of his colleagues has ever come and directly told him that his popularization of science was wrong.

He told interviewer Hal Smith, "It's true that, throughout the history of science, some scientists have been mad at others who popularize, but I've gotten extremely little of that. Why? For two reasons. One, scientists don't do science for conventional rewards—salaries are not high. Scientists get a psychic and emotional satisfaction from doing it. The more people understand the emotional attraction of science, the happier scientists are. One scientist, after seeing an episode of 'Cosmos,' said to me, 'Thank you. You've made me a hero to my kids.' That's the personal reason that scientists favor popularization if it's done well.

"The other reason is that science subsists on public funds, and if the public doesn't know what's happening it is not likely to continue to support it. Fundamental research is funded almost exclusively by the government. Yet the amount of money spent on science is a trivial fraction of our wealth. A lot of scientific research is the seed corn of the future; you can eat the corn and get through one more winter, but then you're dead the following year. I'm hoping 'Cosmos' will make people realize the natural resonance they have with the scientific endeavor."

Or, more pointedly, "Science is a joy. It's not just something for an isolated, remote elite. It's our birthright."

CHAPTER EIGHT

Nuclear Winter

For many years now Carl Sagan has been associated in the public's mind with the optimistic side of science—the exploration of space, the possibility of finding extraterrestrial life, the evolution of life on this planet and elsewhere, and generally the stimulation, fascination, and sheer joy of the quest.

But there has been another side to science in the twentieth century, a dark and frightening side. Modern science has given us the power to destroy ourselves. Sagan recalls that as a boy he first heard of the atomic bomb being dropped at Hiroshima and Nagasaki, but it did not make much of an impact on him. All the news meant to him, and to most Americans at the time, was that the war would soon be over. Sagan first began to think about the real impact of nuclear weapons when he read a science fiction story about what life might be like after a nuclear war.

Sagan has always been interested in science and public policy, but aside from the space program, which he promoted enthusiastically, he had never been closely identified with any major public policy issue until the 1980s. It was then that Carl Sagan and his colleagues discovered the possibility that nuclear war might be even worse than anyone had imagined.

Scientists stumbled upon what has become known as "nuclear winter" quite accidentally and by a rather roundabout route, a common occurrence in the history of science. A scientist may start studying something out of purely intellectual interest and wind up with conclusions that have enormous practical implications.

The starting point for Sagan was the dust on Mars. The *Mariner 9* Mars probe reached the vicinity of the planet in March of 1971, a time when Mars was in the grip of one of its periodic planet-wide dust storms. The orbiting probe had almost nothing to photograph but the featureless dust, and scientists worried that *Mariner* would cease to function before the dust settled. As it turned out, *Mariner* worked better than anyone could have reasonably expected. The dust storm ended in about three months and for the next year *Mariner* was able to provide scientists on Earth with the first detailed look they ever had at the surface of another planet.

But for several months the anxious scientists had nothing to look at except swirling dust. It was a very frustrating time. However, there was an instrument aboard the spacecraft which allowed scientists to take the temperature of the Martian atmosphere at various layers and the temperature of the planet's surface. What the instrument showed was that while the dust swirled, the temperature of the atmosphere was considerably warmer than usual, and the temperature at the surface was considerably cooler. As the storm subsided and the dust settled, the temperature of the atmosphere fell and that of the surface rose to more normal levels.

The reason for this variation from normal temperature was not difficult to figure out. The dust was thrown up high into the Martian atmosphere where it absorbed the sunlight, heating the atmosphere, and preventing the sunlight from reaching the surface. As a result, temperatures on the surface fell. An observer on Mars during the storm would have found the planet becoming increasingly dark and cold.

Sagan and some of his associates, who had little to do until the dust settled, filled their time by calculating how much the Martian atmosphere would be warmed and the surface cooled when a given amount of dust was put into the atmosphere. A few years later, Sagan and his colleagues began applying the same sort of calculations to earthly conditions. The practical aim at first was to find out what happens to Earth's climate when a large volcano erupts. It has long been known that the dust thrown off from major volcanic explosions does produce measurable climatic effects worldwide. The dust from a volcanic eruption in 1815 is believed to have led to an exceptionally severe winter the following year. In Europe it was called "the year without summer," in America "eighteen hundred and froze to death." The methods of calculation developed for Mars seemed to work quite well for earthly conditions.

About that time another group of scientists working on an entirely different problem came up with a theory that also influenced the thinking of Sagan and his colleagues. These scientists concluded from studying 65 million-year-old rocks that the extinction of the dinosaurs and most of the other species of life on Earth in that time was caused by the collision of a large comet or asteroid with the Earth. The collision would have thrown an enormous quantity of fine dust into the atmosphere and created a dramatic, though short-term, cooling of Earth. The climate change, however, would have been severe enough to kill off the dinosaurs and many other types of animals of that time.

Volcanic eruptions are localized events, and even a major one is unlikely to produce catastrophic climate changes. The collision of Earth with a large comet or asteroid is an unpredictable but, fortunately, extremely rare event. But there is a more immediate potential catastrophe—nuclear war. Since the first atomic bomb was dropped on Hiroshima, the public has been aware of the tremendous destructive potential of nuclear weapons. After the development of the hydrogen bomb people knew that the human race possessed the power to destroy its own civilization, perhaps to destroy itself entirely. The theme had frequently been treated in the science fiction of the 1950s which so captivated the young Carl Sagan. The general impression had been that in an all-out nuclear war the destruction would come first from the blasts themselves and then from the radioactive fallout. Climate changes were not considered.

But as the human race and nuclear weapons continued to coexist, people became, if not comfortable with the bomb, at least accustomed to it. The feeling of an immediate threat of a nuclear holocaust was blunted by time. There was also a growing belief, particularly in some government and military quarters, that a nuclear war would be "survivable," even "winnable." Yes, there would be a great loss of life, and a tremendous amount of material destruction but, so this thinking ran, with proper precautions a large number of people (at least in the winning nation) would survive and be able to rebuild their civilization within a relatively short time. The effects of radiation, the nuclear optimists said, would not be permanent, or even that widespread, for most nuclear weapons today are not designed to produce the huge amounts of radioactive fallout that resulted from earlier weapons. Nuclear weapons, some thinking ran, might even become part of "normal" warfare.

Writing in the influential publication *Foreign Affairs,* Sagan noted that some policymakers had dismissed the gloomier claims of the results of nuclear war as "alarmist or, worse, irrelevant . . . The apocalyptic claims are rejected as unproved and unlikely, and it is judged unwise to frighten the public with doomsday talk when nuclear weapons are needed, we are told, to preserve the peace."

As Sagan and his colleagues began to look into the problems of predicting the long-term climatic and ecological effects of nuclear war, they were astonished to discover how little solid research had ever gone into the subject. Many of the conclusions that had been reached in the past were either clearly wrong, based on inadequate data, or heavily influenced by the political outlook of the individuals making the predictions. What was needed was a hard scientific look at all of the possible long-term effects.

With the new data about the climatic effects of dust in the atmosphere, Sagan decided to take that hard look at the possible long-term effects of nuclear war, for it was well known that nuclear explosions throw enormous quantities of dust into the atmosphere. Scientists had speculated rather inconclusively about the subject for years. Work on the climatic effects of nuclear war began in earnest in 1981. About a year later another element was added to the calculations. In addition to the dust, scientists in Germany and Colorado had begun to calculate the amount of smoke from burning forests and cities that might be released into the atmosphere in a nuclear war. Previous investigators had seriously underestimated the fire damage of such a war.

The overall study of the climatic effects of nuclear war was carried out by Richard P. Turco, Owen B. Toon, Thomas P. Ackerman, James B. Pollack, and Carl Sagan. (Both Toon and Pollack had received their doctorates under Sagan's direction.) It became known by the initials of the authors as the TTAPS study. The tentative conclusions of the study were circulated among scientists early in 1983, and stories about it had appeared in some popular newspapers and magazines. A frightening popular article on the scientists' findings appeared in the Sunday supplement *Parade* on October 30, 1983. But a very large percentage of Americans first heard of TTAPS (though they didn't know the name) on the night of November 20, 1983.

Millions had just finished watching a harrowing television drama about the effects of nuclear war called "The Day After." "The Day After" was one of the most heavily publicized and widely watched television shows ever. It was also a very controversial show, for there are those who believe that any discussion of the horrifying effects of nuclear war, any implication that a war is not "winnable," is somehow un-American. The network which produced the show was nervous and had assembled a distinguished panel to discuss publicly the drama and the effects of nuclear war as soon as the show was over. Among the panelists was Carl Sagan. Sagan shocked millions of viewers by grimly announcing that the horrors they had seen dramatized in "The Day After" were probably quite mild when compared to what the aftermath of a real nuclear war would be. "The news," he said, "is even worse."

In "The Day After" most of the main characters who happened to live in the vicinity of a nuclear missile base that is hit during the war were either incinerated immediately when the bombs fell or are shown dying slowly and horribly of radiation sickness. (Actually, the full gruesome effects of radiation sickness were not shown graphically.) There was no adequate medical attention, and food was running out. The viewers were told that similar scenes were being enacted throughout the United States and the Soviet Union. Practically all forms of communication and transportation have ended. Civilization in North America and in the Soviet Union has ground to a halt and may be coming to an end. But the implication is clear that there will be survivors, and the countries that were not involved in the war, particularly those far distant from the nuclear powers, might remain relatively unaffected. From the bleakness the viewer might retain at least a glimmer of hope. The human species will survive.

But then Sagan came along and said that even that glimmer should be dimmed, for based on the TTAPS study, the immense clouds of smoke and dust that would be released by even a medium-scale nuclear war would bring about massive global climate changes and result in a deadly and prolonged period of cold and gloom that the scientists have called "nuclear winter."

Nuclear winter will result when the particles of dust from the explosions and smoke from the fires obscure the sun. Sagan has described the result very graphically:

"On the ground, the obscuration of the sun would in a matter of days cause inland temperatures to drop well below freezing, killing vast numbers of plants and animals. The amount of sunlight reaching the ground would be very low, perhaps too dark for plant photosynthesis. For months there would be a dark, cold, and deadly nuclear winter, no matter what season the war might occur. Most human survivors would starve to death. Even a small nuclear war, involving a mere one percent of the world arsenals, could create enough smoke to cause such catastrophic global changes."

Not only that, but the rising fireball from the nuclear explosions in the stratosphere would produce changes which could destroy the Earth's ozone layer. The ozone layer protects the surface from an excess of dangerous ultraviolet light.

"After a few months most of the particles [of smoke and dust] would settle out of the atmosphere, revealing a defoliated surface still frozen in patches even in the tropics. But the returning sunlight would now include significant ultraviolet light, transmitted all the way to the ground through the depleted ozone layer."

What might the ultimate result be?

"The combination of cold, darkness, radioactive fallout, and ultraviolet light would pose a real threat to the survivors of a nuclear war. The conditions may be so severe and the ecological links so badly shattered that human survival anywhere on the planet would be jeopardized. The extinction of the human species would be a real possibility."

While the total extinction of the human species as a result of nuclear war had always been a popular theme in science fiction, it had quite suddenly jumped from the realm of fiction to terrifying reality.

Sagan's role in moving the theory of nuclear winter from scientific speculation to the forefront of public consciousness was unique. Though he certainly participated actively in the scientific work that led to the formulation of the nuclear winter theory, his calculations perhaps could have been performed by others (although no one had in the thirty-eight years since Hiroshima). No one else could have presented the idea to the American public, indeed to the world, more forcefully, clearly, and believably than Carl Sagan. A public which had become comparatively complacent to the possibility of nuclear annihilation had suddenly been shocked into a new awareness, by the man who had come to be regarded as the chief spokesman for science.

Naturally, a theory as far-ranging as this one has enormous scientific implications. Disputes among scientists can sometimes be fiercely emotional, yet the scientific dispute over nuclear winter has been remarkably low key.

The nuclear winter theory has influenced scientific thinking in a variety of fields, sometimes in surprising ways. Recently some paleontologists have started to complain that nuclear winter has been imposed on the world of dinosaurs. While astronomers and geologists have often been enthusiastic supporters of the idea that the extinction of the dinosaurs was brought about as the result of a collision of some large object with the Earth, and a resulting climatic catastrophe, paleontologists are much less enthusiastic about that theory. The majority of these specialists in ancient life have traditionally believed that the extinction of the dinosaurs was more gradual, and no catastrophes are needed to explain what happened. The evidence of a catastrophic impact some 65 million years ago is quite solid. The controversy is over whether the impact killed the dinosaurs. The argument between the catastrophists and the gradualists has become quite bitter and some paleontologists like Dr. Robert E. Sloan of the University of Minnesota have said, "The nuclear winter theory has influenced some thinking about the dinosaur extinction, just as the dinosaur theory led to the nuclear winter scenario."

Sagan stresses that while the theory of a catastrophic end for the dinosaurs may have helped to influence the development of the nuclear winter idea, the ultimate conclusions about the long-term effects of nuclear war did not depend in any way on the extinction of the dinosaurs. "The dinosaurs could have died of influenza without affecting the validity of our conclusions."

There have, of course, been disagreements as to just how severe a nuclear winter might be, or just how large a nuclear conflict would be needed to set the mechanism for the catastrophe in motion. But scientists from many disciplines agree that the calculations of Carl Sagan and his colleagues are essentially sound, and the prospects of anyone surviving a nuclear war look much bleaker now than they did just a few years ago.

A major study of the environmental consequences of nuclear war by over 200 scientists for the International Council of Scientific Union concluded in 1986: "No new and substantial work . . . has lessened the probability that a major nuclear exchange would cause severe environmental effects."

To some of his critics who claim that nuclear winter is a "worst case" scenario, Sagan replies that he does not believe it is. But also "an argument can be made for worst-case thinking when the stakes are this high. . . . This is not a debate on some arcane point of theoretical physics in which errors, if any, will eventually be corrected by the traditional, tested methods of scientific criticism and debate. Here, if we make a mistake, the consequences may be irreversible."

It is a theory that no one wants to test.

The nuclear winter theory obviously has enormous political implications as well, and the political controversy that has surrounded it has been a good deal fiercer than the scientific one. Though Sagan is neither a politician nor military theorist, he has not hesitated to speak out forthrightly and frequently on these topics. He has spoken to the public, to political issues in the U.S. and other nations, and to the American military and intelligence communities. The possibility of nuclear winter could, and in Sagan's view should, change military thinking.

There is, for example, the theory of a "first strike," that is, that one of the two great nuclear powers suddenly launches an attack on the other in the hopes that the attack will destroy the enemy's capacity to retaliate. But even if such an attack were successful and the attacked country did not retaliate, Sagan believes that the destruction brought about by that first strike might push the world over the nuclear winter threshold.

"We have a reasonable chance that if Nation A attacks Nation B with an effective first strike . . . then Nation A has thereby committed suicide, even if Nation B has not lifted a finger to retaliate."

Countries that were completely uninvolved in the superpower conflict would suffer just as much as the nations that launched the missiles. Do we have a right to decide the fate of the entire world? Sagan asks.

By dramatically reminding people of the terrible consequences of nuclear war, Sagan has drawn the ire of conservatives, who believe that such talk frightens the American public and weakens the national will to resist the Soviets. In general, the conservative philosophy has been that the best way to avoid nuclear war is through increasing America's ability to fight such a war.

This is a notion that Sagan rejects emphatically. In an often angry televised debate with conservative columnist, William F. Buckley, Sagan concluded:

"There is in 1945 a change that happened in the character of weaponry available on the planet. And Einstein, looking at that change, said that everything had changed except our way of thinking. The idea that more nuclear weapons means you're stronger, that more weapons means you're better is a bankrupt and obsolete kind of thinking. The decisions we make in the next few years will determine the future of the human species, possibly; certainly the future of our global civilization. This is not a trivial issue."

There are also those who believe that we needn't worry too much about nuclear war because it's very improbable. After all, they say, we have lived with nuclear weapons for over forty years now and there has been no nuclear war so far. Some even feel that the existence of nuclear weapons has actually prevented major wars.

Says Sagan, "I do not guarantee that this is a perfect anology, but the situation reminds me of a man falling from the top of a high building, saying to an office worker through an open window as he passes by, 'So far, so good.' "

In response to some critics who have said that no nation would be mad enough to start the sort of nuclear war that would result in nuclear winter and that there are too many safeguards to allow such a thing to happen by accident, Sagan wrote:

"The notion that in a crisis national leaders can always be relied upon to behave responsibly or rationally is belied by historical events. It seems likely that had Hitler been presented with nuclear weapons and their delivery systems by 1944 or later, they would have been used even if prompt Allied nuclear retaliation was assured. Chernobyl and

Challenger remind us that highly visible technological systems into which enormous national prestige has been invested can nevertheless experience catastrophic failures. And Hitler and Stalin remind us that madmen can achieve control of modern industrial states or that leaders can become mad in office. The only prudent response, it seems to me, is to arrange a world in which nuclear winter cannot happen . . . to reduce the global nuclear arsenals below the level at which nuclear winter could conceivably occur."

Reducing nuclear weapons is one possible alternative to avoiding nuclear destruction. What about the other suggested alternative, building a defense system against nuclear weapons? President Ronald Reagan, and many in his administration, believe that this is the best way to avoid nuclear war, and have proposed the Strategic Defense Initiative (SDI) or Star Wars. That is a space-based system which would, in theory, destroy incoming missiles, and thus make the U.S. invulnerable to attack, or nearly so. High administration officials have even pointed to the nuclear winter theory as another reason to support Star Wars. The reasoning here is that nuclear war is so deadly that only Star Wars can protect us. By 1986, Star Wars had become the center of a major national and international controversy.

What does Sagan think of Star Wars? Not very much. He has been outspoken in his opposition to the plan. Star Wars, Sagan believes, is nonsense, and extremely dangerous nonsense, to boot. It isn't technically feasible now, or in the foreseeable future to build a reliable shield against a major missile attack. In trying to do so we would spend enormous amounts of money. Some of the estimates, even from Star Wars supporters, go as high as one trillion dollars. Large numbers of scientists and engineers would be diverted from what Sagan sees as more useful research, and ultimately the thing just wouldn't work as protection against attack, because even if it were 90 percent effective the remaining 10 percent of missiles that got through would destroy the country. And even its technically competent enthusiasts do not imagine a shield more effective than this.

In a written debate over Star Wars with Edward Teller, "father" of the H-Bomb, that appeared in *Discover* magazine, Sagan said:

"If absolutely impermeable shields were miraculously emplaced, simultaneously and at reasonable cost, over the U.S. and the Soviet Union, the security of both nations would increase. But the moment the shields are even a little permeable, the moment one is deployed before the other, the situation, I maintain, reverses; then the world becomes much more perilous, and the two superpowers—as well as all the other nations—would be far better off had the shield never been invented."

Sagan believes that the technological problems

facing the construction of a perfect space-based defense system are overwhelming at present. Of course we can never be sure it would work and, short of a war, there would be no way of really testing the thing. Star Wars could be worse than the most expensive technological failure in history; it would fuel the arms race, rather than encourage the reduction of nuclear weapons.

Star Wars will work, say its supporters. There were those who said that we couldn't put a man on the moon, and we did. To such arguments Sagan replies, "The moon did not fight back." Every advance in defense could easily be neutralized by an advance in offensive weapons.

While Star Wars could never be a really effective shield, Sagan believes, it could seriously upset the current shaky balance between the U.S. and the Soviets.

"In Russian nightmares, the United States launches a massive attack on the Soviet Union, destroying much of its retaliatory force. Then Star Wars is used to take care of the much smaller number of Soviet warheads that are launched in retribution."

Sagan does not imply that this is what the U.S. would ever do, merely that it is what the Soviets think that the U.S. *might* do. Thus, at some point Soviet military planners could argue that the only thing to do would be to launch a preemptive strike before the Star Wars system is deployed. This in turn might lead U.S. planners into considering an even earlier strike, and so on. And, of course, even a totally successful strike with no retaliation at all could bring on nuclear winter.

How about the suggestion of sharing Star Wars technology with the Soviets so that both superpowers could build defense systems at the same time, and thus neither side need be fearful or nervous? Sagan finds it hard to imagine that this administration, or any administration, would turn over the most advanced and highly classified technology to the Soviets, and he can't imagine the Soviets ever believing that the U.S. would.

While the possibility of nuclear annihilation is a problem that has been created by science and technology, it can't be solved by them, Sagan believes. "There are no technological 'fixes.' " The only possible solution is negotiation of massive verifiable cuts in nuclear arms by both sides.

If we don't reverse the arms race, Sagan is deeply worried that all of the awesome accomplishments of our species that he has so enthusiastically chronicled, and all of the shining hopes for a future in which we can reach ever farther into space, may vanish in a flash of light and a cold, dusty darkness.

CHAPTER NINE

Contact and *Comet*

Bold speculation, solid scientific accomplishment, science popularization, television stardom; you might think that was enough for a man whose basic work is science. But not for Carl Sagan. In 1985 he launched yet another unlikely project. He wrote a novel. It was predictably science fiction, but it was still a real novel with plot and characters and lots of ideas, not just a piece of science popularization covered by a thin fictional veneer. There have been a few scientists who have written novels. The British writer C. P. Snow was a scientist/novelist, but primarily a novelist. The brilliant and sometimes eccentric British astronomer Fred Hoyle has written some science fiction. Science fiction writer and science popularizer Isaac Asimov long ago abandoned research and teaching for a life of full-time writing. There are few other examples, so Sagan's position as a scientist/novelist is pretty unique.

It was also a pretty exposed position. The scientist as novelist might be open to some heavy criticism for stepping so far out of his area of expertise. The criticism could come from writers or scientists or both. That didn't seem to worry Sagan too much. "What's the worst thing that could happen?" he rhetorically asked *New York Times* reporter Glenn Collins shortly before his novel was published. "That I'd write a crummy novel?"

He told Collins that he had written fiction "for the same reason I've gone on the 'Tonight' show: to reach a different audience, millions of people."

The novel, called *Contact,* had an extraordinary amount of prepublication publicity, not surprising considering the fame of its author. Much publicity centered on the advance, a very hefty $2 million. That wasn't a record advance for a novel, but it may have been for a first novel. The publishers didn't feel they were taking too big a chance; after all, Sagan's nonfiction books had already sold millions of copies worldwide.

The novel, which was published in October of 1985, was not met with the same sort of near-universal enthusiasm and praise that greeted the "Cosmos" series, or many of Sagan's previous books. But it wasn't widely denounced as a "crummy novel" either. *The New York Times* counseled tolerance for Sagan's "many first-novelist vices." "Characterization," said the *Times* reviewer, "proceeds by the dossier method." The writing was "hamfisted in places, precise in others." The reviewer concluded that the book "fulfills no high literary promise." Yet as a novel of ideas, said the *Times,* it succeeds very well because "it does deal with issues seldom discussed and worth pondering."

Politically conservative critics were more upset by Sagan's ideas than by his novelist's skills, or lack of them. "Sagan is blind to the potential consequences of the current crisis of values, even though science's failed attempt to answer the questions of history is one of the principal causes of that crisis," complained Robert Royal in the conservative publication, *The American Spectator.*

Overall, however, the critical reception of *Contact* was quite good. Critics found the plot intriguing and dramatically compelling, the ideas stimulating, and in the end very satisfying. Whatever the critics said, the public flocked to *Contact.* The book spent six months on the *New York Times* best-seller list, and it was one of the ten best-selling books of 1985. Quite an accomplishment for a first novel, even a novel by Carl Sagan.

When the book was reissued in paperback in 1986, it quickly climbed onto the paperback best-seller list. *Contact* is also scheduled to be a major motion picture. In fact, the book originated in a treatment for a motion picture that Sagan and Ann

Druyan wrote in 1980–81. Sagan credits Druyan with helping him with *Contact*. "What I learned from her in the process is what I cherish most about the writing of this book."

It's not wise or even possible to attempt to summarize a long and complex novel like *Contact* in a few paragraphs or pages. It's not fair either, because *Contact* is, in part, a good mystery story, with suspense and a number of genuine plot surprises. To give them away would be to spoil the potential reader's enjoyment of the story.

But there are a number of general themes in the book which do help to illuminate Carl Sagan himself. As you might expect, the book is science fiction about Earth's first encounter with Extraterrestrial Intelligence (ETI)—hence the title *Contact*. The book is not, Sagan insists, his prediction of the future, "but rather the glimpse of a possible future, of which there are many."

The protagonist is radio astronomer Dr. Elizabeth Arroway. This immediately sets the book apart from much science fiction, particularly science fiction written by men, where the protagonist is most often a male, particularly if the character is a scientist. Breaking down sexual stereotypes is one of the ideas that Sagan is trying to get across with *Contact*. Sagan says that the good part of the character of Elizabeth Arroway "is based on Annie."

As a boy, Carl Sagan found the novels of Edgar Rice Burroughs strong on imagination but weak on science. The scientific content of most modern science fiction has improved since Burroughs' day, but there has probably never been a novel with the scientific and technological sophistication of *Contact.*

Way back in 1966 in *Intelligent Life in the Universe,* Sagan and his coauthor had proposed that radio telescopes be used for listening for signals that might originate with an Extraterrestrial Intelligence. He has participated in some of the pioneering though as yet unsuccessful searches. He has spent time at many of the great radio telescope installations throughout the world. There is probably no one who knows what the search is like better than Carl Sagan, or who can explain it more clearly.

The first sign of contact, as Sagan imagines it in his novel, is undramatic, low key and quite unexpected, because there had been so many years of tedium and disappointment.

"His voice trailed off as an alarm light flashed decorously on the console in front of them. On a display marked 'Intensity vs. Frequency' a sharp vertical spike was rising.

" 'Hey look, it's a monochromatic signal.'

"Another display, labeled 'Intensity vs. Time,' showed a set of pulses moving left to right and then off the screen.

" 'Those are numbers,' Willie said faintly. 'Somebody's broadcasting numbers.' "

In the beginning the radio astronomers don't get

too excited because they think it's probably some sort of mistake, a "bogey," or perhaps someone is playing some sort of joke. Things like that have happened many times before. Indeed, incidents of this type have sometimes taken place during the real search for intelligent extraterrestrial signals. So it doesn't pay to get too excited too soon. But with amazing speed the scientists are able to confirm that the signals are indeed both artificial and extraterrestrial. Radio astronomer Arroway's reaction:

"In her mind she thought she could hear one joyous shout amidst a clamor of other voices."

It's not hard to imagine that would be Carl Sagan's reaction to a similar situation.

The story of how the signals are interpreted and how the series of messages hidden within them are unfolded makes up one of the most fascinating parts of the book.

Sagan is not only, or even mainly, interested in giving his readers a fictionalized and easy to digest account of the Search for Extraterrestrial Intelligence (SETI), he has some other ideas he wants to get across. But the details provide a realistic background for the story.

The international nature of science is one of the themes Sagan concentrates on. The message from space can only be deciphered through international cooperation. When the final attempt comes to actually meet the ETIs in person five are chosen, an

American (Dr. Arroway), a Russian, a Chinese, an Indian, and a Nigerian. The most villainous characters in the book are those with the most narrow or nationalistic points of view. Sagan's conservative critics complain that he is too international and not anti-Soviet enough.

There are lots of other themes in *Contact*—the possibility and desirability of physical immortality, the relationship of science and religion, the value of life and of love, and more. The conclusion is sweeping, mysterious but ultimately optimistic about humanity's future and place in the Universe. This overall feeling should come as no surprise to anyone who is familiar with Carl Sagan's other works. *Contact* produces the same sense of awe that one felt when first watching "Cosmos"—just in a different form.

From the time that Sagan first met Ann Druyan and they worked together on the *Voyager* interstellar message project, he has credited her with a good measure of the success of his popular projects—the television series "Cosmos" and the book based on the series, for example. In Sagan's second major 1985 publishing project, Ann Druyan's name is no longer relegated to the acknowledgments page, she is the fully acknowledged coauthor of the nonfiction book *Comet*.

"Along the way a lot of women have done a lot of work for men and got no credit," Druyan told *Times* reporter Glenn Collins. "And here, I'm coauthor of *Comet.*" But Sagan stresses that in every respect she deserves coauthorship. "She wrote a lot of it, especially the best parts."

Druyan is attractive, enthusiastic, and extremely bright. Anyone seeing some of the joint appearances they made promoting *Comet* is aware that she can be every bit as impressive a personality as Sagan himself.

Comet was issued to coincide with the 1986 appearance of Halley's Comet, the most regular and well known of all the visible comets. As far as the general public was concerned, this event which takes place approximately every seventy-six years, was rather a bust. People conditioned by photographs, drawings, and fantasies of previous passages of the comet were expecting something visually spectacular. In fact, the 1986 appearance was one of the dimmest on record. To the ordinary observer, even equipped with a good set of binoculars, Halley's Comet was little more than a barely visible smudge in the sky.

Of course, scientists like Sagan knew that this was not going to be a bright passage for the comet, and warned that people might be disappointed. However, the passage in 2134 should be a really good one.

"That's my 200th birthday," Sagan commented. "I don't know if I'll be around for that one."

The scientists who had been preparing for years for the appearance of Halley's Comet were not disappointed that it wasn't a spectacular light show from the Earth. They were studying the comet with instruments much more sophisticated than a pair of binoculars. Several different types of space probes were launched toward the comet, one passing within a few hundred kilometers of the nucleus itself. The photographs and other data sent back by the spacecraft were spectacular. The 1986 passage of Halley's Comet may have been disappointing to the ordinary ground-based observer, but for science it was the most-rewarding approach of the comet ever.

In many respects the study of this passage of Halley's Comet was an example of international scientific cooperation at its finest. There were probes launched by the Soviet Union, Japan, and the European community. But Sagan was deeply disappointed that the United States did not send a spacecraft to Comet Halley.

He and Druyan wrote, "Several innovative mission designs were proposed by American scientists and engineers . . . But the proposals were turned down by Democratic and Republican administrations both. There was not enough money. The United States had more important things to do. The cost of a major mission to Comet Halley is roughly that of a single B-1 bomber. The United States is committed to 100 B-1 bombers. We couldn't have gotten by with 99."

The main U.S. experiment was to have special

instruments for observing the comet flown aboard the space shuttle. But the disasterous explosion of the space shuttle *Challenger* in January, 1986, made even this modest contribution impossible.

Still, while official and well-funded U.S. cooperation in the scientific study of Comet Halley was poor, plenty of individual U.S. scientists contributed a great deal toward the effort. When the Soviet *Vega* craft neared the comet, Sagan, along with a host of other scientists from around the world, was in Moscow to help interpret the data the vehicle was sending back to Earth. He was also on U.S. television to help interpret those findings for the American public.

Why this apparent obsession with comets? Why a whole lavishly illustrated book about them? Is it merely because the well-publicized return of Halley's Comet grabbed everyone's attention? Is it because there is still a residue of superstitious fear that comets are omens of doom, and Sagan is out to disprove the notion? Both reasons probably figure into his thinking, but his primary reason for being interested in comets is linked to Carl Sagan's cosmic outlook.

Comets are a lot more important than you ever suspected. They are far more numerous than the occasional comet visible from Earth, or even visible to our most sensitive astronomical instruments. There are not billions and billions, but trillions and trillions of them at the outer limits of our solar system. They are, however, billions and billions of years old, having been formed at the same time the solar system was formed. In the cold and dark of space the comets have remained unchanged, except for the occasional erratic one like Halley's Comet which goes careening toward the sun.

The way in which the nature of comets was discovered by astronomer Edmund Halley, among others, tells us a great deal about the scientific method and how it works. It's a remarkable story, and a tribute not only to the power of science to develop and understand the way the Universe works, but to the sheer joy of the scientific quest.

There is a woman in the story, Nicole-Reine Etable de la Briere Lapaute, an eighteenth-century astronomer and mathematician. She was one of those women who did a lot of work for important men and got no credit, at least in her own time.

Comets helped to form the solar system, and they are still helping to change it. Tons of cometary dust shower down upon the Earth every year. Comets created many of the craters on the moon, and on other planets and their satellites in our solar system. It was probably a comet that struck a remote area of Siberia on June 30, 1908, resulting in a blast comparable to a nuclear weapon today. In the more distant past impacts with larger comets may have had profound effects on the history of life on Earth. It may have been a comet that created the catastrophe that killed the dinosaurs 65 million years ago—

and incidentally left the Earth free for the ascendancy of our ancestors, the mammals. Collisions with large comets may also have resulted in other periods of mass extinction earlier in the history of life on this planet. Comets may have even brought to the Earth much of the water upon which life itself depends. Thus, comets may be largely responsible for the origin and direction of life on Earth.

Write Sagan and Druyan; "A surviving dinosaur might have reason to mistrust them, but humans might more appropriately consider the comets in a favorable light—as bringers of the stuff of life to Earth, as ocean builders, as the agency that removed the competition and made possible the success of our mammalian ancestors . . ."

But the enormous destructive potential of comets reminded Sagan and Druyan of nuclear war and nuclear winter. What will the world be like, they wonder, when Comet Halley next appears in 2061?

"At the present rate of change, it seems likely that in the period between now and 2061, the turning point for the human species will have been reached."

If we make it till then, they comment, we should be in pretty good shape for the passage of Comet Halley which will take place in March, 2134. Then the comet should be really close to Earth and be brighter than the brightest star in the sky. Will there be any people around to see it?

So *Comet* is only partially about comets. It is also

an attempt to get us to think cosmically. The trillions and trillions of comets, the billions and billions of years should make our own quarrels here on earth seem petty, and our very existence so tenuous. Yet the human accomplishment in understanding the nature of comets and our potential for knowing far more in the future is truly impressive. Do we also have the sense not to destroy ourselves?

Near the end of *Comet,* Sagan and Druyan note that in past ages the appearance of a comet provoked fear and hope and moved people to prayer. With the reappearance of Halley's Comet they offer their own prayer.

"We live on a fragile planet, whose thoughtful preservation is essential if our children are to have a future. We are only custodians for a moment of a world that is no more than a mote of dust in a Universe incomprehensively vast and old. May we therefore learn to act, before all else, for the species and the planet."

CHAPTER TEN

Toward 2001

In September of 1986, Carl Sagan was arrested at the Nevada Test Site some 60 miles northwest of Las Vegas. He and 168 others, mostly doctors and nurses, were charged with criminal trespass. This act of civil disobedience was part of a protest against continued nuclear testing by the U.S. government.

Sagan's opinions about such issues as nuclear testing were well known. He has opposed it deeply and he has never been shy about expressing his views, or about plunging into the controversy surrounding a whole range of public policy issues. But the kind of activist protest that results in arrest was quite new to him, and very much out of character. "I am," says Sagan "a very law-abiding person."

Getting arrested was a "statement of conscience,"

but not one that he much enjoyed. "I hate it. It's in no way fun," he told the *Cornell Daily Sun*. "It's just that whatever else you're interested in is not going to happen if there's a nuclear war."

Sagan had not gone to the Nevada Test Site for the purpose of committing civil disobedience. He was speaking at a rally against nuclear testing. "The Department of Energy decided it was a good time to advance the schedule of testing. So they blew up a nuclear weapon [underground] right in the middle of our protest. And that helped make up my mind."

Demonstrations are permitted around the Nevada site, but there is a white line, and if you cross it you get arrested. "We crossed, they then handcuffed us, herded us into busses . . . . and then we were all arrested, all done quite politely."

Also arrested was his wife, Ann Druyan. This was Sagan's first arrest. Druyan, who is more of an activist, had already been arrested in an earlier demonstration. It is unlikely that either of them will make a career of this sort of protest, but there is no mistaking Sagan's commitment, and the increasing urgency he feels about the nuclear threat to the survival of our species on the planet.

"I'm neither optimistic nor pessimistic about the future of our species," says Sagan. "We are facing many very serious problems; they were made by us and they can be solved by us—not by exercising complacency and denial, but by attempting courageously to understand our world as it really is (while still remembering how we wish it to be), and by working very hard to improve it. Then we can leave the next generation a world better than the one we were left by the last."

Sagan's next book, tentatively titled *Nucleus* is a nonfiction work about nuclear war. Ann Druyan is writing and producing a show for Public Television's science series, "Nova," called "Confessions of a Weaponeer." The core of the show is a long interview Sagan conducted with the late George Kisitakowsky, a man who played a key role in the development of nuclear weapons and missiles.

Many of the goals which Carl Sagan supports—arms control rather than Star Wars, an end to nuclear testing—are familiar ones, but he has a pet project, which is quite unique to him and which combines the two interests which have dominated his life for years, the promotion of world peace and the exploration of space. This project also harkens back to an interest from his early childhood—going to Edgar Rice Burroughs' Barsoom, the planet Mars. Sagan has proposed a joint U.S. and Soviet manned mission to Mars. The proposal seems a surprising one at first glance, for Sagan has never been an enthusiast for manned space exploration. At the present stage of technology he feels that robots could do the job of space exploration as well as human beings, and that automated missions would be safer and cheaper. But the goal of the Mars mission Sagan proposes would be more than purely scientific. It would also be political—an example of cooperation between the great superpowers. It would be practical, for it would use the technology—rocketry, electronics—that are traditionally used in the arms race. It would engage some of the emotion and the energy that are traditionally unleashed by war. The project would also raise the horizons of the human species, give us all, East and West, something truly inspiring to work on and to think about, something that would help put us above the quarrels that consume so much of life on Earth. It would be one of those "great projects" by which a society, and perhaps our entire species, could be measured.

The technical problems of such a mission, while formidable, Sagan believes, are by no means overwhelming. The project would require no major "breakthroughs." Going to Mars would be expensive, of course; all space projects are expensive. But it would not cost nearly as much as the average person believes. Sagan has written that such a project would "cost far less than Star Wars, less than the Apollo program [the program that sent American astronauts to the moon] and not much more than a major strategic weapons system. In a joint mission, the cost to any one nation would be still smaller."

Sagan points out that with or without the United States, the Soviets have announced they are going to Mars. They have already had extensive experience in keeping men in space for months. The reason, he believes, is to gain knowledge about prolonged weightlessness for the nine-month journey from Earth to Mars.

The Soviets now have a research institute in Siberia which is working on developing closed ecological systems. These are systems in which food can be grown, oxygen generated, and wastes recycled. Subjects have been living in these systems for months. "Reportedly," says Sagan, "occupants are issued only about one-fifth the food they will need, and there is no resupply of water and air, no flushing away of waste products." The development of such systems will be vital in any attempts to explore the solar system. The more food, water, and oxygen that can be recycled within a spacecraft, the more practical space exploration will be.

"A Soviet manned landing on Mars in the early '90s, say, seems unlikely. It is too soon. But a Soviet mission to carry cosmonauts on a close approach to Mars is much easier and just possibly might be launched by 1992. The date is significant—it is the 75th anniversary of the Russian Revolution."

But Sagan notes that 1992 is a year that also has great significance for America; it is the 500th anniversary of Christopher Columbus' discovery of the New World. "What could be more fitting for 1992 than the initiation of an international program for the exploration and eventual settlement of another New World?"

The scope of Sagan's program is characteristically

breathtaking. He has pinpointed 1992 as a good symbolic starting point. That would be the time when the vehicle for the first manned (and womaned, Sagan carefully notes) mission would begin to be assembled in Earth orbit. Assembling the vehicle in orbit would be necessary. Providing the power to lift the entire Mars-bound spacecraft out of Earth's gravity in one shot isn't possible and isn't necessary. The vehicle could be put into space a piece at a time and assembled in orbit by crews of Americans and Russians, cooperating, not confronting one another, "the progress in full view on the evening news," says Sagan.

There will be a flyby of Mars, and perhaps robot vehicles will be landed on the surface. The actual landing of humans on Mars would not take place until the start of the next millennium—that is, around 2001, also a meaningful date.

An American astronaut and a Soviet cosmonaut could set foot on Mars together. "If this really worries us, we can arrange for the ankles of the American and Soviet commander to be tied together."

The symbolic value of such a joint mission would obviously be enormous, but there would be a lot more than symbolism involved. There would be exploration, and experimentation for future expeditions which would have extended stays on the planet. The explorations could be televised back to earth every night. "The wonders of Mars will occupy us for a long time." The voyage would also be the first step in transforming us into a "multiplanet species." This is a step, Sagan feels, that would be as momentous as the descent of our ancestors from the trees ten million years ago.

In the 1960s and early '70s there was a heady excitement about the promise of space, the exploration of the moon and the planets. We seemed on the verge of breaking free from the bonds of Earth and we seemed committed to that goal. More recently, plans have concentrated on the military uses of space—orbiting bombs and "killer" satellites. Sagan is attempting to rekindle the earlier idealism. The U.S. space program, which Sagan says was once "the proudest in the world" is now "the butt of ridicule." His call for cooperation in space and peaceful exploration of distant planets seems almost nostalgic in this era of the Star Wars space defense system and the *Challenger* disaster. Yet the vision is compelling and very refreshing.

For someone whose face, voice, and ideas are so familiar, Carl Sagan is essentially a private man, and despite his fame and fortune, he remains very much the academic—the professor. He is not just another celebrity hawking his latest book or film or political campaign on the talk show circuit. Sagan took a two-year leave to work on the series "Cosmos," and he still does a great deal of traveling throughout the U.S. and the world, attending conferences and giving speeches. But Sagan makes his home in Ithaca, New York, the location of Cornell University.

Sagan's writings and public appearances have

made him a wealthy man. He will never make *Fortune* magazine's list of the richest men in America, but he can afford to live well—and he does. His house is a modern, multileveled cement dwelling balanced on the edge of a gorge in the heights overlooking Lake Cayuga. The view is spectacular. While the house is impressive, the location is not Beverly Hills or the Riviera or other haunts of the rich and famous. This is Ithaca, New York, a university town in the middle of the snowbelt.

The house is guarded by an extensive security system, and iron gates that lock securely. Carl Sagan is too well known to encourage or even allow casual visitors. "I like the isolation. It's hard for people to casually stop by." Fame has its price, and in the modern world the privacy of those who are well known is not respected, and they can sometimes become targets. While he was working on "Cosmos" in California he drove an orange Porsche with the license plate "Phobos." Though he could easily afford the Porsche, he now drives a more modest and less obvious VW Rabbit. It is more the car of a professor than a TV star.

Aside from the two-year period in which he was working full time on "Cosmos," Sagan has never been away from teaching for long. When *New York Times* reporter Glenn Collins visited Sagan in 1985, he found "orange chalk marks streaked his blue suit, the remnant of a session with his graduate students."

For several years after "Cosmos" Sagan abandoned teaching undergraduates. He thought "the words of 'Cosmos' would be echoing in my ears." He concentrated on working with graduate students. But he has now gone back to teaching a small seminar of undergraduates, and he is even thinking about teaching introductory astronomy. "I got itchy to teach undergraduates."

Sagan has developed a senior seminar on "Critical Thinking." He describes it as "essentially about how to equip yourself with a baloney detection kit in an age when the amount of baloney being purveyed is at a recent high."

His research group at Cornell has for several years been doing detailed analyses of some of the data sent back by *Voyager,* and the results of other experiments, in an attempt to duplicate and understand conditions found on the outer planets. "So, for example, for Titan [a moon of Jupiter] we think we have solved the problem of the nature of the mysterious orange-red aerosol that surrounds this world."

This is the sort of hard scientific work that Sagan has been doing all his adult life. But the public knows little of such work, and understands even less. This is a fact which deeply disturbs Carl Sagan. In a talk to the national press club he complained that the press doesn't supply enough hard scientific information. Science is not that difficult to understand, he insists.

Some of the post-"Cosmos" excitement has receded. For a while, Carl Sagan Productions sold a variety of "Cosmos"-related items, like The Cosmic Calendar. But all that has ended. "I'm not temperamentally a businessman."

While life after "Cosmos" has been less hectic, Carl Sagan certainly does not lead a cloistered or quiet life. He may be in Boston one day and Paris the next. There was also a bad health scare in March, 1983. He had an emergency appendectomy which led to serious complications. He was on the critical list for days and very close to death. Though the experience left Sagan looking temporarily gaunt and haggard, he has recovered completely. "I think it possible that this close encounter with death has had something to do with my efforts to help reverse the nuclear arms race."

He's a casual person, and admits to being "not tremendously organized." Sagan's fame and success have given him an unprecedented degree of freedom. He has the opportunity to work on "whatever seems interesting at the moment."

Carl Sagan has three sons by his previous marriages, and one grandson. His oldest son, Dorion, says that when he was a child his father used to make up stories about black holes "and tell them to my brother and me night after night." Dorion adds, "I was probably one of the first people that he experimented on in his attempts to popularize science." Dorion is a skilled magician, a member of the International Brotherhood of Magicians, and a talented science writer. The book *Microcosmos* that Dorion coauthored with his mother, Professor Lynn Margulis of Boston University, received rave reviews. Dorion is also the father of Sagan's first grandchild, Tonio.

Second son Jeremy, a computer software expert, is vice president for research and development for a computer company he helped to found. Third son Nicholas is still in high school and, says Sagan, he "shows considerable promise both in computers and in creative writing."

Sagan's fourth child, with Ann Druyan, is a little girl named Alexandra—whom everyone calls Sashie. Sagan hopefully dedicated his novel, *Contact,* to his youngest child, "who comes of age with the Millennium. May we leave your generation a world better than the one we were given."

The relationship between Carl Sagan and Ann Druyan is a unique one. She is in no sense "the wife" of a famous man, who simply stands behind him and supports him. Nor is she only the collaborator on some of his more successful projects. Though the basic trends in Carl Sagan's thoughts and attitudes have been unchanged throughout his life, his relationship with Ann Druyan seems to have deepened his social concerns and given him more of a taste for political activism.

"I can't imagine a more fulfilling relationship," Druyan told *Times* reporter Collins. "It was years before we knew we were in love with each other."

On New Year's Eve, 1983, Carl Sagan stood before a crowd of about 15,000 people at the Cathedral of St. John the Divine in New York City and delivered what he called "A New Year's Resolution," a talk that he and Annie had written together. They expressed for all of you the same sort of hope they have for the future that Sagan had for his own daughter in his *Contact* dedication.

"Let us act this year, so that in 2001 we can look our children and our grandchildren in the eye and say, 'Here, we made the world a better place for you. We continued the tradition of the 40,000 generations of humans who came before us. Do the same for your children.' "

BIBLIOGRAPHY

Books by Carl Sagan:

–*Broca's Brain: Reflections on the Romance of Science.* New York: Random House, 1979.

–*Contact.* New York: Simon and Schuster, 1985.

–*The Cosmic Connection: An Extraterrestrial Perspective.* New York: Doubleday, 1973.

–*Cosmos.* New York: Random House, 1980.

–*The Dragons of Eden: Speculations on the Evolution of Human Intelligence.* New York: Random House, 1977.

Books by Carl Sagan and others:

–and Ehrlich, Paul; Kennedy, Donald; Roberts, Walter Orr. *The Cold and the Dark: The World After Nuclear War.* New York: Norton, 1984.

–and Druyan, Ann. *Comet.* New York: Random House, 1985.

–and Garwin, R., *et al. The Fallacy of Star Wars.* New York: Vintage Books, 1984.

–and Shklovskii, I. S. *Intelligent Life in the Universe.* San Francisco: Holden-Day, 1966.

–and Bradbury, Ray; Clarke, Arthur C., *et al. Mars and the Mind of Man.* New York: Harper and Row, 1973.

–and Drake, Frank, *et al. Murmurs of Earth: The Voyager Interstellar Record.* New York: Random House, 1978.

–and Leonard, Jonathan. *Planets.* New York: Time-Life Science Library, 1966.

–and Page, Thornton, eds. *UFOs: A Scientific Debate.* Ithaca, N.Y.: Cornell University Press, 1972.

INDEX